A POCKET GUIDE

PRINCESSES OF WALES

DEBORAH FISHER

UNIVERSITY OF WALES PRESS
CARDIFF
2005

British Library Cataloguing in Publication Data
A catalogue record for this book is available from the British Library

ISBN 0-7083-1936-X

Printed in Malta by Gutenberg Press, Tarxien

Contents

Introduction

The concept of a 'Princess of Wales', on which this book is based, is essentially artificial. Before the final conquest of Wales by the English King Edward I, our country was not as we know it now. It consisted of a number of principalities, each with its own prince (and sometimes princess), of which Gwynedd became dominant in the twelfth century. Although the princes of Gwynedd assumed the title 'Prince of Wales', and ruled an area reaching as far as Deheubarth in the south, they did so without prejudice to the claims of lesser lords to be called princes in their own right. Since the last of these native leaders died, in 1283, the title 'Prince of Wales' has been held (mostly) by English princes who had no power or jurisdiction over the people of Wales; in many cases, they never set foot in the country. This does not prevent Welsh people from feeling a loyalty towards the Prince and Princess of Wales, whose existence helps to give them a sense of national identity. Nowhere was this more clearly shown than in the reaction of the Welsh to the death of their most recent princess.

After the conquest of Wales came a long succession of English princes who inherited the title of Prince of Wales. Because of the violence of the power game and the general struggle for survival, they often did not reach maturity, so that there are many gaps in the sequence of princesses between the reigns of Edward I and George I. The 'English' Princesses of Wales, in the first four centuries of the title's existence, were mere pawns in international political games: Anne Neville and Katherine of Aragon are particularly tragic figures. Finally, we emerge into relatively peaceful times and a series of women who prospered along with their husbands, usually ending their lives as queen or queen mother. Paradoxically, it was as their husbands' power diminished that the Princesses of Wales began to have a recognizable role in British society, though even this had little real relevance for those living in Wales.

According to the official royal website, the title 'Princess of Wales' is a courtesy title which applies only to the wife of the Prince of Wales and cannot be used by the eldest daughter of the sovereign, *even if she is the heir to the throne*. Because of the way the princess obtains her title, it follows that she is doomed to remain outside the inner circle of royalty. However much public sympathy she may command, she will always come off worst in a dispute with husband and/or in-laws. Even as queen, her position is far from unassailable. Perhaps only by achieving the status of queen mother can she ever be said to have 'arrived', to be established, a permanent fixture within the current royal family. Only two Princesses of Wales have ever done so.

I once heard a Canadian tourist guide referring to a visit made to his country by Queen Elizabeth II 'when she was Princess of Wales'. His error was clearly prompted by memories of Diana, Princess of Wales. In the context of this book, Diana stands out as an essentially modern woman, not dependent on her husband for either her popularity or her place in society, though her political influence may have been small.

I am not a historian in the true sense, but in researching this book I tried to examine all the available evidence for any statement of historical fact. The problems we face in trying to find out about the princesses of the medieval period are various. To begin with, the mass media did not exist. Caxton's press produced its first copy in 1474, a hundred years after the first 'official' Princess of Wales, Joan of Kent, lived. Although there were written records of contemporary events, those records could only be passed on in manuscript form, with the result that anyone could change or add to them. The writers of 'history', as we call it, were seldom interested in accuracy. They would record any story, or rumour, as if it was a fact. There was nothing to contradict them.

The difficulties are compounded by the fact that the Princesses of Wales were women, a major factor since women did not achieve positions of political power under normal circumstances. No Queen of England had ruled in her own right, either at the time the first English Prince of Wales was created or for two hundred years afterwards. As a result, the actions of men in battle and politics were recorded, but no one was very interested in their wives, mothers, or daughters. This is a pity because, when we study them in detail, we find that most of them had very interesting lives by our standards.

Although physical prowess decreased in importance over the centuries, women continued to be given in marriage as a means of uniting two countries or factions. It is through this medium that many of them managed to influence the outcome of events and play a significant part in history. The women described here may have been influenced greatly by the character and position of their menfolk, but it worked both ways. The difference between this book and others is that it concentrates on *female* contributions to Welsh, and British, history. There are plenty of alternative sources for those who wish to read about great men.

Marriage to the Prince of Wales was described by Buckingham Palace staff as 'the job', in the days before Diana Spencer took it on. Diana herself referred to the royal family as 'the firm'. The pressure on a Princess of Wales to behave in a certain way and fulfil certain expected responsibilities, such as producing an heir, is out of all proportion to what ordinary women face, and this partly accounts for the tragic lives several of them have led. A striking example is Caroline of Brunswick, whose husband, the then Prince of Wales, was petitioning the king for a divorce within a year of his marriage. His father turned him down, saying: 'You seem to look on your disunion with the Princess as merely of a private nature, and totally put out of sight that as Heir Apparent of the Crown your marriage is a public act, wherein the Kingdom is concerned.'

Much the same would be said, over a hundred years later, to Edward VIII, who laboured under the illusion that, as king, he would have greater power to choose than as Prince of Wales. If his choices were limited, how much harder were they for any woman who had, voluntarily or otherwise, undertaken the role of Princess of Wales. Prince Charles, with an endearing naïveté, once remarked in an interview with Wynford Vaughan-Thomas that 'Whoever I choose is going to have a jolly hard job, always in my shadow . . .'

The outline of this book was complete in 1997, when the unthinkable happened and a Princess of Wales died violently. It would probably have been the ideal time to publish, but, while revising the material, I recognized parallels between Diana's life (which I had not meant to include) and those of other 'official' Princesses of Wales, which caused me to think again. The result is a work that highlights the similarities and contrasts between the lives of the later princesses in a way it would not otherwise have been able to do.

When, in 2001, an English-based publisher turned down the proposal for this book, on the grounds that it lacked 'a theme that would tie the book together', I was astounded. At last, a Welsh publishing house has had the vision and commitment to see it through. My experience in seeking a publisher brought home to me the sorry fact that there are still many people in Britain for whom Wales, whether as a principality or as a country in its own right, is an irrelevance. Nevertheless, I believe that I can demonstrate, in the succeeding chapters, how this perception has changed, is changing, and will continue to change.

I found the encouragement I had been looking for, on a website (*www.britannia.com*) which I accessed in my search for additional material. There, historian Peter Williams had noted:

> As far as I know, not a single index in any history book has an entry for Princess of Wales, regardless of whether the title holder was Welsh-born or not. Perhaps future histories (and reference books) will remedy what we now perceive as a glaring omission.

Consider it done!

Some Interesting Statistics

There have been nine 'official' Princesses of Wales since 1284.

Their average age at time of death was fifty-six, the youngest having died at the age of twenty-eight, the longest-surviving at the age of eighty-five. This compares quite favourably with the average age of their respective husbands, which is 50 (excluding the present Prince of Wales, who is 'not out' in his fifties). The average life expectancy of all the 'official' Princes of Wales, including unmarried ones, is forty-seven (again, excluding Prince Charles).

The longest gap between princesses was the period of over 200 years between the death of Arthur Tudor on 2 April 1502 – when his widow, Katherine of Aragon, relinquished the title – and the investiture of the future King George II as Prince of Wales on 27 September 1714, when his wife, Caroline of Ansbach, assumed the title of Princess of Wales. The only time the title has passed directly from one princess to another was in 1901, when it passed from Queen Alexandra to her daughter-in-law, Mary of Teck (although there was officially a gap of ten months between the accession of Edward VII and the appointment of his heir as Prince of Wales).

The youngest Princess of Wales at the time of her marriage was Anne Neville, who was fourteen. The oldest was Joan of Kent, who was thirty-three.

Four of the nine princesses were born in Britain, three in Germany, one in Denmark and one in Spain.

Six of the nine eventually became queen, but only four of these graduated directly from Princess of Wales to the higher title. The remaining two were previously married to Princes of Wales who died before achieving the throne. In all, six of the nine outlived their princes. Only two ever became queen mother.

The longest-serving Princess of Wales was Alexandra of Denmark, who held the title from her marriage on 10 March 1863, until she became queen on 22 January 1901. The princess who held the title for the shortest period was Katherine of Aragon, who held it from her marriage on 14 November 1501, until her husband's death on 2 April 1502 (when she became Princess Dowager of Wales).

The most married Princess of Wales was Joan of Kent, who was married three times in all. Four of the nine princesses endured estrangement, annulment or divorce at some time during their lives.

The Princess of Wales who gave birth to the most children was Caroline of Ansbach, who had ten, eventually dying of a ruptured womb.

Only one of the nine princesses did not die of natural causes.

PART I

Memorial to Gwenllian, daughter of Llywelyn the Last.
Photo courtesy of the Princess Gwenllian Society.

Before the Conquest

Before describing how the title of 'Princess of Wales' developed under English rule, we shall take a look at the Welsh princesses who lived prior to 1282. Many of these are known by name, but few of their lives are adequately recorded by history. This is partly because there were so many. The daughters of Welsh chieftains or minor princes had been given in marriage since Roman times, and even earlier, as a means of cementing alliances and retaining the integrity of family inheritance. That was normally the beginning and the end of their perceived significance as people.

The word 'princess' means nothing more than the daughter, or daughter-in-law, of a monarch or ruler. The territory that ruler commands may be anything from an empire to a tiny principality. (As it happens, the Spencer family estate is the size of Monaco.) There is not much to link the early princesses except their social position relative to other women of their time and locality. Sometimes this restricted their options, but no more than for other women, few of whom had even the imperfect kind of freedom the female sex enjoys today. In general, however, these women were at the top of the social ladder. Their marriage partners were carefully chosen, and their conduct, if it departed from what was expected, could have disastrous results. Those that are remembered by history are often remembered precisely for this reason.

Angharad, daughter of the eleventh-century prince, Owain ab Edwin, and wife of Gruffydd ap Cynan, is one of the first Welsh princesses whose name we know. Her importance in history, as with so many of these medieval women, rests largely on the identities of her father and grandfather, her husband and her son.

Likewise, the notorious beauty, **Nest**, mistress of King Henry I, is remembered for her scandalous conduct in eloping with a cousin from under the nose of her Norman husband, at Cilgerran Castle. As a result, she became known as the 'the Welsh Helen of Troy'. Gerald of Windsor was not a forgiving person, and his men sought out and killed his love rival five years later. How much of this thirst for revenge was due to Gerald's affection for his wife, and how much to simple male jealousy and loss of face? Nest's part in Welsh history is not insignificant, but as usual it is limited to the context of her marriage and childbearing. We need to look further afield for women worthy of their royal titles.

Cristin, second wife of the great Owain Gwynedd, has had a bad press because she encouraged her own children to fight their half-brothers for control of Gwynedd. The Welsh tradition of dividing a father's property equally between all his sons, whether legitimate or not, had led to bloodshed on countless occasions. Cristin wanted her sons to prevail over their elder brothers simply because the alternative was for them to put themselves at risk. Apparently not content to be the wife of a great man, she wanted to steer her destiny, and that of her sons. Owain had found a partner worthy of him. Owain was not an arrogant man; he never called himself Prince of Wales, and his wife was never called Princess of Wales.

Neither was Owain's sister, **Gwenllian**. We have already met her mother, Angharad, but she pales into insignificance in comparison with Gwenllian, whose father, Gruffydd ap Cynan, had dominated north Wales for sixty years. With such antecedents, it is hardly surprising that she showed such indomitable spirit, yet for a woman to take the action she took against the Normans in 1136 was extraordinary. Gwenllian's husband, Gruffydd ap Rhys, ruled only a very small area of Deheubarth, and was always looking for an opportunity to regain his lost inheritance. Despite some military success against the Normans in Ceredigion, he had been forced to travel north to seek assistance from his father-in-law. Meanwhile, Maurice de Londres, lord of Kidwelly, moved to put down the rebellion of Hywel ap Maredudd in the south. The impetuous Gwenllian decided to take the initiative herself. Together with Morgan and Maelgwn, two of her four sons, she led her husband's men into battle against Maurice at Kidwelly, where they were defeated on the field known as Maes Gwenllian

(Gwenllian's meadow). Morgan was killed and Maelgwn captured by the enemy. Gwenllian herself was decapitated in the battle.

It is not difficult to see the motivation for Gwenllian's actions. Brought up by a father who had fought hard and ruthlessly to win back his own inheritance, she had been made to live in the shadow of her less illustrious husband. It may have been her intention to prove herself to him as well as to safeguard her family. She must have underestimated the skill and strength required to lead an army, and it is hardly surprising that she failed. She must have been a modern-minded woman, anxious to show the men of the family that she could do anything they could do. She should have taken note of Boudicca's fate. Gwenllian's exploits are remembered, and she has become symbolic of Welsh resistance to English rule, an icon for modern nationalists who comes more readily to mind than her namesake, Gwenllian of Gwynedd.

The immediate forerunners of the 'English' Princesses of Wales were themselves mostly of English and/or Norman blood. It was Llywelyn Fawr who started the trend, in the early thirteenth century, when he agreed to take as his wife **Joan** or Joanna, an illegitimate daughter of King John of England. Intermarriage between Norman nobles and the local aristocracy had happened in Wales before this date, but not within the royal house of Gwynedd. The Welsh court must have been a daunting place for a girl in her early teens, even a king's daughter. She had to attempt to learn the native tongue (though the educated classes were able to converse in Norman French). Her own name was translated into Welsh as 'Siwan'. Her illegitimacy would at least have been no handicap. Llywelyn's own illegitimate sons were allowed by Welsh law to inherit his lands, and had to be given equal rights with any legitimate children he might later father.

Siwan's son, Dafydd, was to be Llywelyn's successor, after much wrangling with his older half-brother. Siwan, accustomed to English ways as well as ambitious for her natural son, would have encouraged Dafydd to think of himself as the heir, and he was the first to take the formal title Prince of Wales. Llywelyn himself had taken only the title Prince of North Wales, and was described by the English as Prince of Aberffraw and Lord of

Snowdon. Llywelyn had long recognized the dangers of allowing a father's property to be evenly distributed among his sons, and his action in making Dafydd his heir was a significant departure from Welsh tradition and legal practice.

Siwan played an important part in the diplomatic affairs of her husband's realm. After King John's death, Llywelyn's profitable relationship with the English crown continued. In 1221, at Shrewsbury, Siwan's son Dafydd was recognized as Llywelyn's sole heir by King Henry III, Siwan's half-brother. Things suddenly turned sour in 1230, when a Norman lord, William de Braose, was hanged by Llywelyn, reputedly for being discovered in an affair with Siwan. If adultery occurred, it is curious (to modern eyes at least) that William's daughter Isabella de Braose nevertheless became the wife of Siwan's son Dafydd and hence Princess of Wales (strictly speaking, the first) until his untimely death in 1246. However, if adultery with Siwan was not the reason for de Braose's execution, it is equally difficult to see why none of the Marcher lords attempted to intervene on his behalf, or why Siwan herself was imprisoned until 1232. It appears that Llywelyn forgave her publicly for her part in the affair, an unusual action for a powerful man and perhaps one of political expediency. Yet, when she died in 1237, all sources are agreed on Llywelyn's genuine sorrow. Siwan is a real curiosity, and the subject of much creative fiction. Her subservience to her husband, under whose guidance she had grown from a child to a woman, seldom prevented her thinking and acting for herself. She was called Lady, rather than Princess, of Wales, but she deserves her place in history, as a woman who might have been capable of ruling in her own right.

Llywelyn ap Gruffydd, who inherited the title, Prince of Wales, from his uncle, Dafydd ap Llywelyn, had no known illegitimate children (who would, under Welsh law, have been his heirs). Llywelyn was an ally of Simon de Montfort, though their only common purpose was to curb the power of the English Crown. At the height of his success, no one foresaw that de Montfort would be defeated and killed at the battle of Evesham in 1265, and all his family banished from the realm. Llywelyn, as Simon's ally, had already pledged to marry his daughter Eleanor before Evesham, and did not go back on his promise. Their betrothal and proxy marriage took place while she was living in France with her mother and the Welsh prince no longer had anything to gain by this association with a disgraced family.

Eleanor's mother died in 1275 in France, leaving her only daughter in need of protection, and Eleanor prepared to travel to Wales. While approaching her new home by sea, her ship was captured by 'pirates' off the Scilly Isles, and she found herself the prisoner of King Edward I, who was furious that Llywelyn had not asked his permission to marry. It was not until January 1278 that Llywelyn was allowed to correspond with Eleanor, after paying homage to Edward and making territorial concessions. On 13 October 1278 the couple finally married, in Worcester Cathedral, with the king and queen in attendance. Edward himself shouldered the expense of the celebrations; but, immediately before the wedding, he had forced Llywelyn to sign an extradition treaty.

Despite the twenty-year age difference, Eleanor and Llywelyn enjoyed a few blissfully happy years of marriage. Resentment continued to fester among the Welsh, as disputes were settled, under English law, in favour of English lords. During this period Eleanor wrote at least three letters to her cousin, the king, under her new title of Princess of Wales and Lady of Snowdon. In 1282, Eleanor finally gave birth to that long-awaited child, Llywelyn's only heir. Unfortunately for him, not only was the baby a girl (whom he named Gwenllian), but the wife who had brought joy to his middle age died in the process. This was the end of Llywelyn's dreams of a united Wales free from English rule. Stunned by Eleanor's death, he allowed himself to be pressurized by his brother Dafydd into another rebellion against the Crown. He died a few months later in a skirmish at Irfon Bridge.

In Wales, as in England at that time, Gwenllian could not have ruled in her father's place even had she remained his only heir. This did not prevent Edward I from taking steps to ensure that she could not become a symbol of Welsh resistance or be married off to some ambitious opportunist. Gwenllian was sent to a Gilbertine convent at Sempringham in the east of England, where she remained until her death fifty-four years later. The king claimed to be taking the step out of pity, and in order 'that the innocent and unwitting may not seem to atone for the ill-doing of the wicked'.

The importance of 'what might have been' was such that legends grew up about Gwenllian's subsequent fate. It was said that she had been rescued from the convent by some gallant noble and lived a more glorious life under another identity. The truth is well attested. The royal family were well aware of her existence, and, in a gesture that smacks of guilt, King Edward III, grandson of the man who sent her there, awarded her an annual pension. In 1337, following her death, Piers Langtoft wrote of her as 'full courteous' and much loved by her fellow nuns. It may be regarded as a sad end for Wales's ruling dynasty. It is more comforting to think that Gwenllian, known to her English adopters as 'Wencilian', may have found fulfilment in the cloisters of Sempringham, and did not hear too much of the tragic history of the parents she never knew.

Although she made no impact on history during her life, Gwenllian of Wales has since become an icon, representing the durability of the patriotic spirit of Wales. The Princess Gwenllian Society, formed in 1993, has erected a memorial to her on the site of the former Sempringham Abbey, and there has even been a proposal to make her birthday a national holiday. Her death marks the end of any hopes of an independent royal dynasty for Wales, but not the end of national pride.

PART II

Ludlow Castle, where the English kings set up a Council of Wales to be presided over by their eldest sons. Photo © Rhys Jones, LRPS.

After the Conquest

Since the demise of the last Welsh Prince of Wales in 1283, the title of Princess of Wales has been held by the wife of the reigning monarch's eldest son. Their number is not great, and Diana, Princess of Wales was only the fourth since the fourteenth century to have been born in the British Isles. That she was actually able to boast some, very diluted, Welsh blood (she was directly descended from Henry Tudor) perhaps gave her a better claim to the title than most of her predecessors.

King Edward I's wife, Eleanor of Castile, liked to accompany her husband on his campaigns, and gave birth to his son at Caernarfon Castle in north Wales on 25 April 1284. The story goes that, a few days later, the king promised his Welsh critics a new prince to replace the one whose lands and titles he had recently usurped. The replacement would be one born in Wales, who spoke not a word of English. After receiving their eager assent, he produced his infant son, the future Edward II. The boy was known thereafter as Edward of Caernarfon; but the story is apocryphal, having been first written down in 1584 by an unreliable antiquary, David Powel.

Since the child was not at the time of his birth the heir to the throne, it is unlikely that his father would have lavished such an honour on him, let alone such a responsibility. King Edward invested him with the title of Prince of Wales only when he turned sixteen. By then, he was the eldest surviving son, and the title was certainly more appropriate for his having been born in Wales – one of only three kings of England who would ever claim this privilege (the others being Henry V, born at Monmouth, and Henry VII, born at Pembroke).

The present Prince of Wales's official website – he is, of course, the first Prince of Wales to have one – points out that 'the role of

The Prince has not been defined over the centuries. It has always been for each Prince of Wales to interpret his position as he wishes'. This is misleading. The role of the Prince of Wales has more often depended on the wishes of the reigning monarch than of the heir apparent.

Although Edward I had appropriated the title of Prince of Wales for his son, the first Princess of Wales was not his son's wife, Isabella of France, since they did not marry until the younger Edward had succeeded to the throne. There has been a relatively small number of Princes of Wales since 1283 (Prince Charles being the twenty-first) and a large proportion have failed to reach the throne. Several who were eligible for the title were never invested with it, and, of those who were, only about half married in time to share the honour with a princess.

The title Princess of Wales was unknown to the medieval Welsh, let alone the English. It was Dafydd ap Llywelyn who would first proclaim himself Prince of Wales. His wife, Isabella de Braose, daughter of a Norman noble, had a low profile, and bore no children. The next possible claimant, Eleanor de Montfort, enjoyed her status as wife of the Prince of Wales for only about four years. There was never a princess who ruled in her own right in the Welsh principalities. Until the time of Mary Tudor, it was as unthinkable for a woman to rule Wales as for a woman to take the throne of England.

The most recent debate on the nature of the title of Princess of Wales took place on the coming of age of our present queen, Elizabeth II. Elizabeth had become the heir to the throne through the unexpected accession of her father, George VI, and a family discussion apparently took place as to whether she should receive the title of Princess of Wales. The king rejected the idea, though he could not think of an appropriate title to give her in its place. His grounds for rejection were, firstly, that the title, Princess of Wales denotes the social rank of a wife of a Prince of Wales, and, secondly, that there would be no suitable title for her consort. (The princess was shortly to marry Prince Philip.)

Wynford Vaughan-Thomas, in his 1982 book on the princes of Wales, may not have been aware of this episode, but commented: 'In these days of Women's Lib, we note with interest that no woman has ever been created Prince of Wales – or should we say, Princess? – in her own right . . . The medieval mind did not take kindly to the idea of women leading armies.'

Just as each Prince of Wales has tackled the role differently, so each of the princesses in this book has been constrained by the peculiar circumstances of her taking the title. Mary Beacock Fryer, in her book on the subject, comments: 'In a very real sense, each woman who has held the title was a product of her own era.' Although the succeeding pages demonstrate the truth of this, they also reveal how similar some of their experiences were.

*Joan of Kent, the first Princess of Wales after the conquest,
encourages her son, the young King Richard II.
From a Victorian print.*

Joan of Kent (1328–1385)

It was appropriate that Joan, wife of Edward, the 'Black Prince', should have been the first official holder of the title of Princess of Wales. Through her mother, Margaret, Joan was a direct descendant of Llywelyn the Great, Prince of Gwynedd, whose legitimate granddaughter, Hawise, had married Baldwin Wake, Margaret's paternal grandfather. Joan was also the Countess of Kent in her own right, and is known to history as 'the Fair Maid of Kent', underlining her reputation for dazzling beauty. Her husband never succeeded his father on the English throne, but Joan's son would become the ill-fated King Richard II.

Joan's progress to a royal title was highly controversial. Aged thirty-three (two years older than the prince) at the time of their wedding, she had already been married twice and had four surviving children. One of her former husbands was still living. These circumstances aroused the disapproval of the king and queen. Joan had the charisma and enjoyed the popularity that we have come to associate with successive holders of her title. If Caroline of Brunswick was the Diana of her day, Joan of Kent was the 'Fergie' of hers.

She was born in September 1328 at Arundel, Sussex, the daughter of Edmund, Earl of Kent. The earl, a son of Edward I by the latter's second marriage, was executed by his sister-in-law, Queen Isabella, and her lover, Roger Mortimer (a member of the powerful Marcher dynasty which had played a signifi-cant role in Welsh history). Edmund's crime had been to support his deposed half-brother, Edward II. Only when the youthful Edward III reached his majority would Mortimer and Isabella be brought to book.

The earl's widow was left with four children. Her younger daughter, Joan, was only two years old. For a brief period after her husband's execution, Margaret and her fatherless children were prisoners at Salisbury Castle, home of the Montague family, into which Joan would later marry. As soon as the battle for the monarchy was over, Margaret's nephew by marriage, Edward III, took responsibility for her and her children, and looked after them well. Thus the Prince of Wales and his future princess were cousins who knew one another from infancy.

Amongst her extended family, Joan was known by the pet name Jeannette and the prince, named Edward after his father, remained fond of her into adulthood. At Christmas 1348 he made her a gift of a silver beaker, possibly part of the spoils from his soldiering in France. Queen Philippa, renowned for her tender-heartedness, may have made a favourite of Joan at first, but, as her son grew older, she became concerned about the budding romance between the two cousins.

Joan has been described as 'something of a character'. This is an understatement; Joan set a precedent for scandalous behaviour. Her first legal marriage took place in 1341, when she was only thirteen. Her husband was William Montague, son of the Earl of Salisbury, whom she married under pressure from both their families. As an interesting aside, the marriage made her, nominally, a queen, since her husband had inherited all his father's titles, including the kingship of the Isle of Man, received in return for loyal service to King Edward I. Needless to say, he never visited the island.

Unknown to Joan's family, she was already committed elsewhere at the time of her wedding to Montague. As Countess of Salisbury, she moved in the highest society, numbering the king himself among her many admirers. By all accounts, she was a striking woman, with her perfect features, auburn hair that reached to her waist and dark eyes. The French chronicler, Froissart, described her as 'la plus belle de tout le roiaulme d'Angleterre et la plus amoureuse' ('the most beautiful woman in all the kingdom, and the most tender'), and the Herald of Sir John Chandos (a friend of the Black Prince) called her 'Une dame de grant pris, Qe belle fuist, plesante et sage' ('a lady of great worth, who was beautiful, pleasant and good'). Joan was regarded as a leader of fashion, even before her elevation to princess, her style of clothing being described as 'daring' and 'extravagant'.

An annulment was obtained in 1349, after Sir Thomas Holland came forward with the claim that he had entered into a clandestine marriage with the countess 'by mutual consent before witnesses' a year before her union with Montague. Holland claimed he had then departed on crusade, and had been unable to prevent her being married off to his rival in his absence. Whatever the truth, he convinced the pope of his rights in the matter. Joan's legal husband, learning of the affair, kept her a virtual prisoner while the enquiry was in progress, because of her intention to support Holland's claim. In fairness to Montague, there is room for doubt about exactly when Joan's liaison with Holland began. She enjoyed a certain standard of living, and the fact that Holland had made his fortune abroad must have inclined her in his favour. Following the annulment of her marriage to the earl, she married or remarried Holland and lived with him until his death in 1360. Of their five children, four survived into adulthood, and the Prince of Wales was godfather to two.

The popular though probably apocryphal story of how the Order of the Garter came to be founded has given rise to the suggestion that Joan may at one time have been mistress to Edward III himself. In around 1347, when Joan was still living with the Earl of Salisbury, a banquet was held in Calais to celebrate recent military successes. The belle of the ball was, according to Froissart, 'the Countess of Salisbury'. The king promptly claimed her as his dancing partner. In the process, the lady's blue velvet garter somehow ended up on the floor, elastic not being available in the fourteenth century. The king is alleged to have picked it up and placed it on his own leg, saying, 'Honi soit qui mal y pense' ('Evil be to him who thinks evil of it'), the motto of the new order of knighthood.

As Joan was Countess of Salisbury at about this time, it is often assumed that she was the woman in the case, but her mother-in-law, Katherine Montague, who had held off the king's determined assault on her virtue some years earlier, seems a likelier candidate. There is no other evidence to link Joan with the king romantically, though Edward was a notorious womanizer. If the story is true, it is ironic that in 1348 the Black Prince headed the roll of names of the first Knights of the Garter. Another of their number was Joan's husband, the Earl of Salisbury.

It was in 1353, during her marriage to Holland, that Joan inherited the title of Countess of Kent on the death of her younger brother, making her a very eligible widow when Holland died. She had been only a few months without a husband when the Prince of Wales approached her to plead the suit of his friend, Sir Denis de Brocas. Reputedly, Joan refused on the grounds that her heart was given to another and for this reason she would never marry again. This was the prince's cue to ask who the mystery lover was, and Joan replied coyly that it was none other than himself. We can imagine how she allowed the 'secret' to be wheedled out of her.

Their wedding took place in October 1361. It was said that the king and queen (or, more probably, Queen Philippa alone) disapproved of the union. This cannot have been because they disliked Joan, though they may have had concerns about her reputation. Their disapproval probably sprang partly from their preference for an alliance with another royal family. To make matters worse, the archbishop of Canterbury warned the prince that doubts might be cast on the legitimacy of any children Joan might bear him, in view of the fact that one of her previous husbands was still alive. The marriage went ahead only with an assurance of absolution from the pope.

In 1337, the Black Prince received the title of Duke of Cornwall; the duchy was ever afterwards to be associated with the Prince of Wales. He was not formally invested with the latter title until 1343, when he was in his early teens. We must remember that this was only the second time the title had been conferred on a king's son, and it was not regarded as automatic. As Prince of Wales, Edward was nominal head of a council of twelve members, which was the final arbiter in legal decisions affecting Wales. The prince appears to have taken an active part, often signing the orders with his own hand. However, the income he received from Wales was not great, when we consider that with it came the responsibility for maintaining peace within the principality. Historians have noted the heavy-handedness of the royal approach. In 1343 Edward III proposed that the prince's investiture should be marked by the repair of some of the Welsh castles – at the expense of the people of Wales. This suggestion was poorly received. In 1348 the prince sent officials to his principality to make sure that the correct taxes and rents were being collected, evidence that his subjects were not entirely satisfied with English rule.

The Black Prince, by this time having 'won his spurs' at the battle of Crécy, only ever visited the Welsh borders in person to recruit archers for his French campaigns. These he kitted out in a distinctive green-and-white uniform, mainly to enable the English to recognize that these speakers of a foreign language were on their side. Wynford Vaughan-Thomas described the Welsh as 'the Gurkhas of their day', with a reputation for being hardy and tough. One of the prince's favourite knights was Sir Hywel ap Gruffydd, nicknamed Hywel y Fwyall (Hywel of the Axe), wielder of an enormous battleaxe.

In his 1959 book on the princes of Wales, L. G. Pine wrote that in this period 'the prince was educated in the traditional manner of a prince: to govern his future people . . . The education of the prince was such, in actual experience, of responsibility, as would fit him to govern his realm.' Following their marriage, however, in 1363, the prince and princess departed not for Wales but for Aquitaine, a royal possession which they were to rule on the king's behalf. The Prince of Wales had recently also been invested as prince of Aquitaine. England was in the middle of the territorial dispute with France which came to be known as the Hundred Years War; this explains why this piece of the kingdom, so far removed geographically, in the heart of Europe, should have been deemed more important than Edward's other principality. The prince and princess remained in Aquitaine for eight years, living in a manner appropriate to their status.

The Hundred Years' War was at its most vicious, but the blood of the French and English royal families was closely inter-mingled. In the midst of the English court, a Frenchman, Jean de Froissart, was writing his own account of the times, recollecting his time 'in the service of Queen Philippa when she accom-panied King Edward and the royal family to Berkhamstead Castle to take leave of the Prince and Princess of Wales . . . I heard an ancient knight expounding some of the prophecies of Merlin to the Queen's ladies. According to him, neither the

Prince of Wales nor the Duke of Clarence, though sons to King Edward, will wear the Crown of England, but it will fall to the House of Lancaster.' The prophecy would come true, as Froissart knew by the time of writing.

The Prince of Wales's court in Aquitaine alternated between Angoulême and Bordeaux. The Chandos herald comments: 'There abode all nobleness, all joy and jollity, largesse, gentleness and honour . . .' Human nature being what it is, many will have disapproved of the extravagant lifestyle enjoyed by the prince and princess, a view that would echo down to the twentieth century. The royal marriage, one of the happiest in history, was blessed with a son, Edward, in January 1365. A lavish tournament was held to celebrate the birth, with 18,000 horses in the prince's stables for the duration. The future Richard II arrived two years later, becoming his father's heir when his elder brother died in 1372.

It was around this time that the familiar crest of the Prince of Wales's feathers began to be used. The battle of Crécy in 1346 had made the Black Prince (then only sixteen) his military reputation. At that battle, the blind King John of Bohemia was killed, and his plume of three ostrich feathers was allegedly bequeathed to the prince. The fact is that such an emblem was popular, and King John had no monopoly on it. Heraldic experts say the feathers may have originated in the family of Prince Edward's mother, Philippa of Hainault. The King of Bohemia did, however, pass on his motto: 'Ich dien' ('I serve'). We also know that Joan owned a bed of red velvet embroidered with silver ostrich feathers. The use of the emblem was not confined to her husband and son, but was common to all the sons of Edward III.

Fighting remained at the top of the Prince of Wales's agenda. It was his greatest talent, and when he was involved in a military campaign he worried less about his family than they did about him. By 1367 the Castilian ruler, Pedro the Cruel, an ally of England, had fallen on bad times and was rescued by the Black Prince. Pedro was so grateful that he made the Prince and Princess of Wales a present of an impressively decorated round table. Joan accepted it reluctantly, allegedly saying: 'I fear lest ill come of it. The present is beautiful but it will yet cost us dear.'

The Black Prince was drawn into a war he could ill afford, and marched off just as his wife was giving birth to their second son at Bordeaux. Prince Richard was born on the feast of Epiphany, and by coincidence there were three kings present – those of Castile, Navarre and Majorca. This caused a local astrologer to predict that Richard would be the next king of England. The auspicious circumstances would not have been much distraction for the princess, who was preoccupied with worry over her husband. Just to add to her concerns, her eldest surviving son from her first marriage, the teenage Thomas Holland, was also in the army.

The ensuing battle, at Montiel, was one of the Black Prince's greatest victories, but Pedro was killed, and there was no money to pay the troops. In the meantime, the Princess of Wales was forced to raise another army, because the prince's enemies were threatening Aquitaine in his absence. She successfully repelled the would-be invaders. Our impression of Joan during this period is that she was a gutsy lady as well as an attractive one. No doubt she had the confidence that goes with wealth and good looks, but she was not without troubles.

The princess's elder son died at the age of six, leaving Richard as his father's heir; and the Black Prince *needed* an heir. The scourge of the French, victor of Crécy and Poitiers, was a sick man. By 1371, he declared himself unable to perform his duties as Prince of Aquitaine, and returned to England. It was a miserable time for the whole country. The plague wreaked havoc in the homes of humble and mighty alike, killing Joan's mother in 1372. Joan inherited Margaret's title to add to all the others, becoming Lady Wake of Lidel. In the same year, the Black Prince forced himself to attempt one final, abortive campaign in the hope of saving his father's French possessions. His health was now completely shattered. To everyone's surprise, he was well enough to attend the opening of Parliament in 1376. Later the same year, a week short of forty-six, he died in bed at Westminster.

Joan's son, Richard of Bordeaux, was now heir to the throne. It had been his father's dying wish that the boy should be created Prince of Wales, no doubt more as a gesture to his own memory than anything to do with the principality. Whatever the reason, the title was quickly bestowed by the king on his grandson. Richard was only nine, and Joan, the dowager Princess of Wales, became the most influential woman in the country. Her mother-in-law, Philippa, had died of dropsy while the prince and princess were in Aquitaine. In 1376, after the Black Prince's death, one-third of the revenues of the principality of Wales was granted to his widow, but Joan surely relished her position as the first lady of the kingdom more than material possessions.

After a marriage which, though not long by today's standards, was a very happy one, Joan must have grieved for the loss of her husband. Nevertheless, she continued to play an important part in public life, as mother of the heir apparent, and had no female rival. Richard, only the third English prince to be formally invested as Prince of Wales, was soon to take the throne, still in his minority. Following his investiture, late in 1376, he was sent to preside over a new Parliament in place of his grandfather. It fell upon the bishop of St David's to introduce him. This was no more than a lucky coincidence.

History tends to concentrate on the military successes of Edward III's reign, overlooking the civil unrest that was close to the surface during his last years. Much of the controversy focused on John of Gaunt, Duke of Lancaster, a younger brother of the Black Prince. Gaunt shared with his sister-in-law a sympathy for the religious reformer, John Wyclif, who was due to come to trial, and took a small army along to the proceedings to ensure that Wyclif was fairly treated. These events resulted in a riot outside Gaunt's London residence. He was forced to take refuge with Joan at Kennington, and it was largely thanks to the Dowager Princess of Wales that a resolution was negotiated. Within months, her son Richard was King of England, and would rely heavily on his uncle for guidance.

These were dangerous times. The Peasants' Revolt of 1381, led by Wat Tyler, threatened to bring down the ruling classes. The Lollards, Wyclif's followers, had enjoyed Joan's protection, but the violent climax of the popular movement for reform would reduce the feisty dowager to a state of terror, whilst leaving the young king with an improved reputation.

Most of the rebels came from the southern and eastern counties of England. In June, returning from a pilgrimage to Kent, Joan encountered the Kentish contingent on the road.

They briefly arrested her, but allowed her and her women to continue their journey unharmed, their motive being to retain the king's favour. However, another group later broke into the Tower of London, where Joan was taking refuge, and searched her private quarters. One is reputed to have tried to kiss her, whereupon she fainted. This does not sound like the same woman who had helped her husband defend Bordeaux against the French and flirted with kings at state banquets.

Richard, on the other hand, seems to have inherited an indomitable spirit from both parents. At the age of fourteen, he distinguished himself by his statesmanlike approach to the situation; the revolt was quelled and Tyler killed.

As King of England, Richard II was not a success. Some people put this down to his having more of his mother's character than his father's, but he had been influenced as much by the prince's absenteeism as by the princess's presence. In 1382 another woman began to compete with Joan for her son's attention. Richard's new queen was Anne of Bohemia, a meek young woman who, left to herself, would have been easily overpowered by her mother-in-law. Richard, immature as he was, developed an extraordinary devotion to her.

Joan did not hold the title of queen mother, because she had never been queen. She remained the Princess of Wales, but a dowager princess. Although no longer the focus of her son's attention, she was apparently able to call on her daughter-in-law's influence with the king to save John Wyclif from execution for heresy, following the publication of his *Confessio*. In later attempts to influence the outcome of events she was less successful.

In 1385 Sir John Holland, Joan's younger son by her secret teenage marriage, was campaigning with Richard in Scotland when a quarrel broke out between him and Lord Stafford, a court favourite. Stafford was killed and Holland was condemned to death. The idea that one of her sons might be killed by another must have been terribly distressing to Joan. She pleaded with the king for four days to spare his half-brother. On the fifth day, she died. She was just short of her fifty-seventh birthday. Richard, stricken with remorse, pardoned John Holland, who duly departed on a pilgrimage of penance. Later, he would return as a leader of the nobility in the troubled times that surrounded Richard's adult kingship, eventually losing his head to the axe under Richard's successor.

Froissart adds an extra twist to the tale. When Henry Bolingbroke had usurped the throne and held Richard a prisoner, he taunted the deposed king with the claim that he and his elder brother were not in fact of royal blood, having been fathered on Joan by an unknown courtier, possibly a priest. Her motivation for such recklessness was her failure to produce heirs by her husband, the Black Prince, and a consequent fear of divorce.

This accusation does not hold water. The Black Prince was clearly capable of fathering children, having already produced a couple of by-blows, and Joan's fertility could not be called into question. More to the point, the Prince and Princess of Wales had been married less than three years when she became pregnant for the first time, and much of the intervening period had been spent travelling. There was no reason for Joan to have been so anxious about the lack of children as to risk taking a lover. History therefore gives no particular credence to this version of events.

It is the only point in the story at which Joan's colourful history may be said to have been a disadvantage to her, or at any rate to her son. Despite initial warnings about her past and contemporary criticism of her lifestyle, she was one of the most successful Princesses of Wales ever to hold the title. Whether her past would have caught up with her had she become queen is a question on which we can only speculate.

An immediate result of Richard's death, in 1400, was that a new leader of Wales came to the fore to challenge the new king. For a period, there were two Princes of Wales. One, recognized by the English, was Henry of Monmouth, son of King Henry IV. The other, recognized by the Welsh (and the French), was Owain Glyndŵr. Wales suddenly had a high profile. The whole country was up in arms, and represented a serious security risk, so there was more awareness among the English that they had not completely eradicated the Welsh identity. That factor would become more important in the period leading up to the Wars of the Roses.

The Interlude:
Margaret Hanmer (c.1370–c.1420)

In a curious interlude at the beginning of the fifteenth century,
Wales once more found itself with a native prince and princess;
it is only right that they should be mentioned in this book.
Owain Glyndŵr, a disgruntled nobleman descended from the
princes of Gwynedd, suddenly revived Welsh nationalism by
rebelling against the English Crown. His immediate motivation
was a dispute over property with a powerful noble, but the
results of his actions were far-reaching. So effective was his revolt
that he was recognized by several foreign governments (those
which were traditional enemies of England) and held parlia-
ments at Machynlleth and Harlech.

Owain's wife, Margaret, is never referred to by the history
books as Princess of Wales. She is seldom referred to at all, even
in biographies of her husband. The Hanmers were an important
family of the Welsh borders, with estates in Shropshire and
Flintshire. Their line has continued right up to modern times.
Margaret's father, Sir David Hanmer, was a judge of the King's
Bench, and this has led to conjecture that Owain had legal
training. In 1381 Sir David was appointed joint justiciar (or
governor) of south Wales. Although the Hanmers were of English
stock, Sir David had married Angharad, daughter of a powerful
local family, and was accepted as part of the Welsh com-
munity. His daughter was referred to in the Welsh way, as
Marred ferch Dafydd (Margaret, daughter of David).

The couple were married in about 1383, when Owain was in
his late twenties and Margaret probably at least ten years
younger. This was well before the dispute with Reginald Grey
of Ruthin which caused Owain to revolt against King Henry IV.
The new bride could not have foreseen that her husband
would one day proclaim himself Prince of Wales; so it would

not be surprising if she never came to see herself as a princess. She remained very much in the background, even during the heyday of Owain's military and political success.

For the first fifteen years of her married life, she was the wife of a gentleman of property. After military service, Owain had built new houses on the estates inherited from his father. Margaret was a lady (what we might think of as a gentle-woman or a 'county' woman) respected by her neighbours, leading a comfortable existence in her husband's ancestral home at Sycharth, near Oswestry. Much of what we do know about their life together comes from poems written by bards of whom Owain was a patron, notably Iolo Goch and Gruffydd Llwyd.

The bards do not draw a clear portrait of Margaret, giving instead conventionally complimentary descriptions such as 'gwraig orai o'r gwragedd' ('best of all wives') (Iolo Goch) and 'merch eglur llin marchoglyn' ('daughter of knightly stock'). By all accounts, the couple's home was furnished with such modern conveniences as were available at the time, and there they enter-tained not only bards, but people of quality from far afield. Iolo describes the house on the hill, surrounded by a moat, with an orchard, a vineyard, a deer park and acres of farmland. According to the poet, Owain and his wife kept open house 'and very rarely were the latch and lock seen in use'.

Margaret's father died in 1387, which was unfortunate for her but would save Sir David from ever having to make a choice between family and career. Even without him, she retained import-ant family connections. Her mother's brother was Maredudd ap Llywelyn Ddu, and her mother's sister had married John Kynaston, steward of Maelor Saesneg and Moldsdale. Her broth-ers, Gruffydd and Philip, were among those who proclaimed Owain Prince of Wales in the year 1400.

For Owain to throw up his enviable lifestyle in order to assert Welsh independence in the face of a usurper speaks volumes about the strength of his patriotic feeling, but his wife's reaction may have been less enthusiastic. By now she may have had as many as eleven children, called by the poet 'a beautiful nest of chieftains'. She was probably raising Owain's illegitimate children along with her own, medieval Welsh attitudes to relationships

Harlech Castle, last stronghold of Owain Glyndŵr, where his wife, Margaret, and children were captured. Painted by Henry Gastineau (1791–1876).

being more liberal than modern ones or even contemporary English ones. Owain, as the best surviving claimant to the throne of Gwynedd, had become a focus for the discontent of his fellow countrymen, and it was as much this as his own grievances which led to his rebellion, in which he was supported by all three of his brothers-in-law as well as his wife's two uncles.

Ian Skidmore, Owain's distant relative and biographer, describes him as a psychopath who enjoyed killing. This, contrasted with what little we know of his home life, suggests a split personality who probably did not give his wife an easy time. The most interesting men are often those whose zest for life makes them difficult husbands, and we can never know how happy their marriage was.

As a result of Owain's early victory against an English army at the battle of Bryn Glas in 1402, Edmund Mortimer, the surviving grandson of Lionel, Duke of Clarence and hence descended from Edward III, fell into Welsh hands. Mortimer, who had an excellent claim to the throne of England, was taken prisoner in the expectation of obtaining a ransom from Henry IV. However, the king saw Mortimer as a potential danger almost as great as Owain himself, and neglected to negotiate his release.

The result was that Mortimer changed sides, allying himself both with Owain Glyndŵr and with his brother-in-law, Henry Percy ('Harry Hotspur'), son of the Earl of Northumberland, in what became known as the Tri-Partite Indenture. Their stated purpose was to restore Richard II (at the time the public could not be certain whether the late king was dead or alive) to the throne; but this was a thin disguise for the trio's plan to divide up the whole of England and Wales between themselves. To cement the alliance, Mortimer married Catrin (Catherine), the daughter of Owain and Margaret, becoming their son-in-law in November 1402. The young couple had at least three children, including a son, Lionel, before Mortimer's untimely death in 1409.

Meanwhile, Owain was widely recognized as Prince of Wales. His allies included the King of France; and Margaret's brother, John, was appointed ambassador to the French court. John would be captured by the English in 1405 and fined for his part in the insurrection. He got off rather lightly, compared with the rest of his family.

Things ceased to go Owain's way. Percy was killed at the battle of Shrewsbury in 1403, before the fruits of the triple alliance could be enjoyed. Owain's home at Sycharth, where he had held court, and his other house at Glyndyfrdwy were razed to the ground by Owain's rival, the young Prince Henry, whose growing military brilliance represented the final nail in the coffin of Owain's ambition. For the woman who had spent many years turning the house into a comfortable family home, this must have been a major blow. History, as usual, makes no mention of Margaret's reactions.

It is not certain whether Edmund Mortimer's death was a violent one or the result of plague, but it occurred during the siege of Harlech by the English. Keeping a low profile had not prevented Margaret Hanmer from becoming a pawn in the political game. When Henry of Monmouth, the official (and Welsh-born) Prince of Wales, looked for a way to bring the rebel leader to heel, he needed to look no further than Margaret and her children, taking them hostage following his victory at

Harlech. Catrin was now a widow; the ages of Margaret's other children are unknown, but Margaret may herself still have been of childbearing age. The fate of the captives was unhappy. Four years after their transportation to London, the death of Catrin and her daughters is recorded. The date and nature of Margaret's death is unknown, though she was still alive in 1413, when her daughter and granddaughters were buried. Owain himself had escaped capture, but was never seen in public again.

The second of Margaret's daughters, Alice, married Sir John Scudamore or Skidmore, a Glyndŵr sympathizer who lost his official position under the terms of a peculiar statute of 1401 which stipulated that anyone married to a Welshwoman could not hold public office. It is in one of the couple's houses on the Welsh borders, Kentchurch in the Monnow Valley or Monnington Straddel in the Golden Valley, that Owain Glyndŵr, following his forced retirement, is believed to have ended his days in about 1415. Other daughters were Janet, probably married to Sir John Croft; Margaret or Mary, married to a member of the Monnington family of Monnington-on-Wye; and Isabel, married to Adam ap Iorwerth.

The eldest of Owain's and Margaret's six sons was probably Gruffydd, who is known to have died in prison. At least one son, Maredudd, survived and was eventually pardoned in 1421, long after his father's disappearance. The Welsh royal line might not have been completely wiped out; but homegrown resistance to English domination would cease to make itself felt. Margaret Hanmer became, literally, a footnote in history. No Welsh-born woman would ever hold the title of Princess of Wales again.

Anne Neville at her coronation. From a Victorian print.

Anne Neville (1456–1485)

Just as most queens of England never held the title of Princess of Wales, so several of the Princesses of Wales never became queen. The next 'official' princess after Joan of Kent was Anne Neville, the daughter of Richard Neville, Earl of Warwick, known to history as 'the Kingmaker'. Though Anne eventually became queen, it was not as a result of her marriage to Edward, Prince of Wales. Anne's life story in fact contains not one, but three, Princes of Wales named Edward.

Known as Edward of Westminster, Anne's first husband was the son of King Henry VI and Margaret of Anjou and would become the only Prince of Wales to die in battle. Unkind contemporaries threw doubt on his true parentage; the boy's father was renowned for his piety and popularly believed to be incapable of fathering a child, but there is no evidence of Margaret's having had an intimate relationship with anyone else. The rumours were fostered by Yorkist supporters, whose own claimant, Richard Plantagenet, had been heir to the throne until the prince's birth.

Whatever the truth, by the time Edward was born in 1453, Henry was incapable of taking any interest in his son and heir. He had been seized with another bout of the mental illness from which he would never fully recover. It was around this time that another family, the Tudors, made their first appearance on the scene. Their story would be closely entwined with that of the Plantagenets from now on. Henry VI's French mother, Katherine of Valois, separated from her child shortly after his birth, had gone on to marry a Welsh courtier, Owen Tudor, and had a further four children before dying tragically young. Henry, on coming of age, could not make amends to her for the shabby treatment she had suffered at English hands, but he bestowed

earldoms on two of his half-brothers, an act that had important consequences for the future of the British monarchy.

For the time being, the youthful Richard Neville, Earl of
Warwick, had an interest in ensuring that the claims of the
Yorkist heirs to Henry's throne were not superseded by the
existence of a new Prince of Wales. It was through his machin-
ations that armed strife broke out between the rival houses of
York and Lancaster, leading to the king's being deposed in
favour of his distant cousin, Edward IV. (Like Edmund Mortimer,
Edward IV was descended from Lionel, Duke of Clarence.) Henry
VI, who presented no physical threat to the new dynasty, was
imprisoned.

The Earl of Warwick was a family man. His younger daughter,
Anne Neville, was born at Warwick Castle, the family seat, in
June 1456, but spent much of her childhood at Middleham
Castle, one of her father's northern residences, where the Neville
Gate can still be seen. Here, Anne must have known the children
of Richard Plantagenet, whose claim to the throne had initiated the Wars of the Roses. Plantagenet was killed at the battle of
Wakefield in 1460; Edward IV was his eldest son. His youngest,
Richard, was nearest in age to Anne, and entered Warwick's
household in his early teens, remaining there until he came of
age and was able to acquire a home of his own. Warwick's
castle at Sheriff Hutton, like Middleham, would one day come
into Richard's hands.

With Edward IV on the throne and the Earl of Warwick in
favour, the way should have been clear for the earl's daughters,
Isabel and Anne Neville, to marry according to their station and
affections. However, the new king was in love with Elizabeth
Woodville, a widow and a commoner. The Earl of Warwick expected Edward to take his advice and keep Elizabeth as a
mistress while marrying a foreign princess. Warwick set sail for
the Continent, to negotiate a suitable bride. As soon as his
back was turned, Edward married Elizabeth Woodville. Warwick
was furious. It looked as though the Woodville family would
be the new power behind the throne.

Having no sons to succeed him, Warwick needed to attach
himself to the royal family that promised most, regardless of

whether it was Yorkist or Lancastrian. Repressing his annoyance over Edward IV's choice of wife, he married his elder daughter, Isabel, to the king's younger brother, George, Duke of Clarence (eventually to die mysteriously, reputedly by being drowned in a vat of malmsey). King Edward's preference for his new in-laws continued. When in 1470 it became clear that Warwick had lost the influence he craved, the earl split with the Yorkist faction and travelled, with the equally discontented Clarence, to Calais, where they joined the exiled Margaret of Anjou. The remainder of Warwick's family followed.

Anne Neville's elder sister, Isabel, had been given to the Duke of Clarence in the hope of maintaining her father's hold over the Yorkist monarchy; Clarence's father-in-law had nevertheless lost the king's favour. Warwick was hedging his bets, and he had only one more daughter to give away. The marriage of his younger daughter to Queen Margaret's son took place in December 1470, at the Château d'Amboise, confirming the earl's new allegiance to the house of Lancaster. It was probably the idea of Louis XI of France, the Spider King, a cunning man who was no friend to Edward IV; Margaret is said to have needed some persuasion. Distrusting Warwick, she insisted he prove himself by taking an active military role on her behalf. The couple remained in France as guests of René of Anjou, Margaret's father, while Warwick returned to England and succeeded in restoring Henry VI, temporarily, to the throne.

Up to this time, the Prince of Wales's only acquaintance with his principality had been as a fugitive from the Yorkists earlier in the war. In 1460, after the battle of Northampton, he and his mother had been sheltered by the Welsh for a time before travelling by sea to Scotland, in those days a separate kingdom. Wales continued to be, for the most part, staunchly Yorkist up to the end of Edward IV's reign. This allegiance can be largely attributed to the glories achieved by thousands of Welshmen who served under the Black Prince and were loyal to his son, Richard II (whose deposition had started the long-running feud between York and Lancaster). There were pockets of Lancastrian resistance within Wales. Denbigh Castle was held temporarily by Jasper Tudor (one of Henry VI's half-brothers), and Harlech Castle was the last Lancastrian stronghold in the country, falling to the Yorkists only in 1468. With the income from the principality already given away to the Plantagenets, Margaret had become desperate to save her son's inheritance.

There remains doubt as to whether the marriage of Anne Neville and the Prince of Wales was solemnized or consummated. Anne was never officially known by the title of Princess of Wales but this proves nothing. She might equally have taken the title on betrothal or on marriage; it is not easy to draw the line between engagement and marriage in this period of history. Furthermore, the title was still a novelty, having been previously held by only one English princess. If so eminent a historian as Simon Schama can refer, on television, to Joan of Kent as the queen mother – a title which, never having been queen, she could never have held – then it is hardly surprising if people who lived a century after Joan's death had forgotten that there was such a title as Princess of Wales. The failure to honour Anne with the title may also reflect the fact that her husband Edward had a rival as Prince of Wales. Richard Plantagenet's grandson, another Edward, was born to Edward IV and Elizabeth Woodville towards the end of 1470 and was in effect Prince of Wales from his birth.

What we know for certain is that Anne and Edward were living together after the ceremony at Amboise. Shakespeare's version of the story, in which they appear a happy couple, need not be taken at face value. Even without the complication of Tudor propaganda, it is known that playwrights of that era were more concerned with effective drama than with historical fact. Contemporaries give no grounds for supposing that the Lancastrian Prince of Wales and his bride were unhappy, but they cannot have spent much time alone together, since Margaret of Anjou would not rest until she had brought the conflict between York and Lancaster to a conclusion. It was a conclusion that turned out bitterly for her. Margaret, whom we imagine as the stereotype of the domineering mother-in-law, was a determined and ruthless woman, who inspired devotion in her followers. History labels her 'the tigress of France', but she went on the offensive only to protect the rights of her son.

Philippe de Commines, a diplomat in the service of King Louis of France, sums up the circumstances succinctly in his *Mémoires*:

> This was a strange marriage! Warwick had defeated and ruined the prince's father, and then made him marry his daughter. He also wanted to win over the Duke of Clarence, brother of the rival king, who ought to have been afraid lest the Lancastrians regained their position. Such events can never happen without dissimulation!

We can always rely on Commines for the common-sense view. He tells how a lady-in-waiting advised the Duke of Clarence not to trust Warwick, warning that 'he should consider very carefully whether Warwick would make him King of England when the earl had married his daughter to the Prince of Wales and had already done homage to him'.

Clarence (who must have been rather dense to need these facts pointed out to him) took heed and defected. When the Prince and Princess of Wales returned to England in April 1471, they were greeted with the devastating news that the Earl of Warwick had been defeated and killed at the battle of Barnet, and Edward IV was once more king. With the loss of their military mastermind, their campaign had little hope of success. Margaret's army failed to cross the Severn into Wales, where she had hoped for asylum, and was forced to give battle without having received the hoped-for reinforcements in the form of Jasper Tudor's men.

The Prince of Wales met his end at Tewkesbury, near the Welsh border, where he is buried in the abbey church. One chronicler asserted that Anne was with her husband when he was brought into the king's presence, after the battle was lost, and murdered; this is undoubtedly false. On Edward's death, or even before the end of the battle, Margaret and Anne, with their female attendants, took refuge locally, possibly at Paynes Place, Bushley. They are believed to have ended up at a religious house in Malvern, whence they were retrieved and brought to London, according to some accounts, in the train of the victorious Edward IV. Malvern Priory has a window given by Richard, Duke of Gloucester and Anne Neville, after their marriage, perhaps in gratitude. At this time in Anne Neville's life, the possibility must exist that, unlike her predecessor and most of her successors as Princess of Wales, she may have crossed the Welsh border. Whether she would have been aware of it, and, if so, what her attitude to it would have been, are questions no one will ever answer, and perhaps the answers are not of much importance.

One version of the subsequent story describes how Anne, bereaved and expecting Yorkist retribution, concealed herself by masquerading as a common servant in a poor area of London. The king's youngest brother, Richard, Duke of Gloucester, later to be reviled in history as King Richard III, rescued her, later marrying her and making her his queen. Other accounts state that she was sent immediately to Middleham Castle, now Richard's property. In either event, Anne and Richard seem to have been married before the end of 1472, though the exact date is not known. She must have given up any thought of ever becoming queen. Her new brother-in-law, Edward IV, was still in the best of health, and besides his two sons and several daughters, there was George, Duke of Clarence, who was married to Anne's elder sister, Isabel. Clarence was restored to the king's favour, and would have sons in due course.

We must not think of Anne as having been lumbered with an ugly, physically deformed second husband whom no self-respecting woman would touch with a bargepole. The only known portraits of Richard show a dark-haired, average-looking man, and written accounts give a picture of someone smaller than his brothers, possibly with one shoulder slightly higher than the other, but certainly not hunchbacked as described. Where Richard's present-day supporters go wrong is in assuming that, just because some of the stories about him have been proved untrue, all of them must be false.

After Tewkesbury, which temporarily put an end to Lancastrian hopes of regaining the throne, Clarence had been forgiven for his defection to Warwick, and the king had restored his possessions, including the inheritance of his wife, Isabel Neville. This was a cause for grievance to Richard, who had remained loyal through thick and thin. A lasting disagreement between the two younger brothers followed, as they fought for control of the Beauchamp estates which the Neville sisters had inherited through their mother. (Anne Beauchamp remained in sanctuary at Beaulieu, from where she wrote to every influential woman she could think of, bemoaning her fate and begging for assistance.) How this controversy affected the relationship between Anne and Isabel is not clear. Clarence had inherited the earldoms of Warwick and Salisbury through Isabel, as well as the lands formerly owned by her father, Warwick the Kingmaker. Because of his continuing jealousy of Richard, the king also gave him the office of chamberlain, which had been Richard's.

Anne was, with her sister, co-heiress to her mother's estates (including the lordship of Glamorgan), but it is questionable whether Richard had any ulterior motive for marrying her, especially after her father's disgrace and death. He was the king's trusted brother, governor of the north of England, and Warwick's lands north of the Trent had been given to him after the battle of Barnet. An order of Parliament gave Richard the right to enjoy Anne's inheritance even in the event of their divorce; but there is nothing to suggest that such a divorce was contemplated. Agnes Strickland, writing in 1851 when it was still fashionable to regard Richard III as a monster, suggests that it may have been Anne who sought a divorce; again, there are no grounds for this. It is more likely that an annulment was feared on the grounds of consanguinity, Richard and Anne being related both by blood and by marriage.

Clarence was incensed by the idea of their marriage, and probably tried to prevent it. The king constantly found himself acting as an intermediary between his brothers. Shortly after the wedding, Anne's mother was able to leave Beaulieu, and placed herself under Richard's protection, but, as Paston wrote, 'the Duke of Clarence liketh it not'. The newlyweds had grown up together at Middleham, where they now made their home, and there seems no doubt that Richard was very attached to Anne. She soon became the mother of yet another Edward, future Prince of Wales, sometimes called Edward of Middleham after his birthplace. Unfortunately for Anne, he was the only surviving child of her marriage. His exact birth date is disputed, but fell somewhere in the years 1473–6. We cannot put the blame for Anne's infertility on Richard, who had fathered several illegitimate children. Anne's elder sister, Isabel, by contrast, gave birth to four live children during her short marriage, but died in 1476.

Clarence's bad conduct over the years following the king's generosity led to Richard's regaining some of what he had lost. Richard was not Clarence's only enemy – he had managed to fall out with the Woodvilles. After Isabel's death, Clarence misbehaved again, ending up in the Tower on a charge of treason, and this time there was no forgiveness to be had. Dominic Mancini, an Italian recording his visit to England, states that Richard deplored Clarence's secret execution in 1478, despite the bad blood between them. Mancini's account was written for the benefit of the French intelligence services, and was not available to historians until the twentieth century. Whatever the truth, Edward of Middleham gained the title of Earl of Salisbury and Richard was restored to the office of chamberlain. With both parents dead, Clarence's surviving son was given into the care of his aunt, Anne.

Anne enjoyed eleven years as Duchess of Gloucester before her husband seized the throne of England. The second half of this period was spent largely at home in the north of England. A war was raging between England and Scotland, and Richard, as commander of the army, spent little time at court, but probably also did not spend much time with his wife. Through Anne, Richard had come into possession of Barnard Castle, and made many improvements to this property, including a new bakehouse and brewhouse. It became the headquarters of the Council of the North. At Middleham, perhaps under his wife's influence, Richard founded a 'college', a religious establishment. In his lordship of Glamorgan, he granted a charter to the chapel of the Holy Cross at Cowbridge, and the nearby Llanblethian church is also traditionally associated with Anne.

Richard was also a patron of Queens' College, Cambridge, which had been founded by Anne's former mother-in-law, Margaret of Anjou, and patronized by her new sister-in-law, Elizabeth Woodville. Anne was later recognized as co-founder, and, in return for royal gifts, the college prayed daily for Richard, Anne and their families. In 1484, as king and queen, the couple would visit the university to receive its gratitude in person.

Edward IV died quite suddenly, aged only forty, and the throne passed to his elder son, who became King Edward V at the age of twelve. Edward IV had taken more interest in Wales than most of his predecessors, and had created a new Council of the Welsh Marches, based at Ludlow, where he had sent his son to learn the craft of kingship. It was there that the prince was residing when the news of his father's death reached him; it was on his way back to London that his entourage was intercepted by Richard, Duke of Gloucester. Richard's plans were not immediately obvious; he had been appointed official protector to his brother's children. When Dominic Mancini comments that 'the Welsh could not bear to think that, owing to their stupidity, their prince had been carried off', he unconsciously reveals that the title of Prince of Wales had come to mean something to the Welsh people even if it meant little to its holder.

Within two months of his nephew's accession, Richard, in what seems a scandalous abuse of his position as protector to King Edward V, had both the young king and his brother declared illegitimate, on the grounds of their father's supposed secret marriage to another woman before Elizabeth Woodville. Just to be on the safe side, he added the accusation that his late brother, the king, had probably been illegitimate himself. It is ironic that Richard's motive for this outrage appears to have been the fear that the Woodville clan would effectively run the country during the king's minority. The Woodville influence was precisely what had caused Anne's father to go over to the Lancastrian cause thirteen years before.

So much has been said and written about King Richard III that it would be pointless to discuss him at length. Our interest is in Anne Neville and how she coped with her sudden elevation to queen consort. Her husband's character may throw some light on their married life, but is otherwise irrelevant. Their coronation took place with full speed at Westminster Abbey, where preparations had already been in the making for the ceremony on behalf of the boy king whose place Richard had taken. Anne's clothing included 'four and a half yards of purpille cloth of gold upon damask' and sixteen yards of Venetian lace. An eyewitness observed that 'Queen Anne had both earls and barons preceding her. The earl of Huntingdon bore her sceptre, viscount Lisle the rod with the dove, and the earl of Wiltshire her crown.' She was, it seems, the first queen consort to be allowed to bear a sceptre and rod. Following the coronation, the king went on a solo progress around England, meeting up again with his wife to enter York in state.

Though she had been a princess before, to find herself once again in the limelight may not have sat well with Anne's home-loving personality. Her main interest was surely in the welfare of her small family, and the loss of her son may well have caused the deterioration in her own health. Her inability to produce more children suggests that she may have been of a frail disposition to begin with.

Like his predecessors, Edward of Middleham met an early death, at the age of about ten, within a short time of his investiture as Prince of Wales, an event which took place at York Minster in September 1483. After their accession to the throne, Richard and Anne continued to spend time in the north of England, the source of Richard's military strength throughout his short reign. It is probable that Edward's delicate health had prevented him from attending his parents' coronation in London in July, but the rapturous reception they received from their 'home supporters' in the city of York led to the decision to hold the lesser ceremony there. It seems to have been a last-minute decision, judging by the records of large quantities of fabric and coats of arms being ordered at short notice from the King's Wardrobe. That there was never any question of the investiture being held in Wales underlines the emptiness of the prince's new title. It did, however, carry with it a substantial financial allowance. The letters patent by which the prince was invested declare him to be a boy of 'singular wit and endowments of nature', a conventional flattery.

Then tragedy struck. In April 1484, in his parents' absence, Edward died suddenly at Middleham. According to the Croyland Chronicle, when the news was brought to them at Nottingham, 'you might have seen his father and mother in a state almost bordering on madness by reason of their sudden grief'. Anne, not surprisingly, showed more outward sign of grief than her husband. The chronicler declares that 'neither society that she loved, nor all the pomp and festivity of royalty, could cure the languor or heal the wound in the queen's breast for the loss of her son'.

The prince was buried in the parish church of Sheriff Hutton. Edward, Earl of Warwick, orphaned son of the Duke of Clarence and Isabel Neville, was now pronounced heir to the throne, which was rightfully his in any case. Anne, being his aunt by blood, was probably responsible for this move; that idea is supported by the fact that Richard named a different heir following her death. However great her affection for her nephew, it could never equal what she had felt for her own son.

Anne did not long survive her boy. Perhaps mercifully, she died in March 1485, before seeing her husband defeated and killed by Henry Tudor's invading army at the battle of Bosworth. In the last few months, her health was in such a poor state that rumours were already circulating about the likely identity of Richard's next queen. It was even said that he intended to marry his own niece, Elizabeth of York, to whom Anne had shown special favour, inviting her to celebrate Christmas at court. Great significance was read, by some observers, into the fact that the two women were wearing dresses of the same cloth.

If there was any truth in the rumours, Richard's probable motive would have been to neutralize the opposition by snatching Henry Tudor's preferred bride from his grasp and at the same time ensuring that any future children of his own were also the rightful heirs of Edward IV. Sir George Buck, an otherwise reliable seventeenth-century historian and an apologist for Richard, claimed to have seen a letter from Elizabeth of York herself to the Duke of Norfolk suggesting she knew of such a scheme.

Contemporary accounts suggest that Anne was only too painfully aware of her imminent death, which took place at Westminster and was marked by a solar eclipse. Like her sister, she was prone to ill-health, and probably died of tuberculosis. After the event, the rumours which circulated were even worse than those that had gone before, it being said that Richard had poisoned her.

Shakespeare, a hundred years later, made Anne appear to Richard as a ghost the night before the battle of Bosworth, with the words:

> Richard, thy wife, that wretched Anne thy wife,
> That never slept a quiet hour with thee,
> Now fills thy sleep with perturbations . . .

In reality, Anne's husband grieved openly at her death, of which he was almost certainly innocent.

Richard III was a competent and popular king, but this does not alter the fact that he deposed his own nephew, whom he had sworn to protect. Those who favour his memory have tended to suggest that all the stories about his propensity to murder were invented later by the Tudors, but this does not hold water. (I will not choose this moment to introduce the question of the kind of racial prejudice which leads some to assume that the English Richard could not have done something so beastly as to murder two children, therefore the crime must have been committed by the Welsh Henry.)

Philippe de Commines, whose reliability has already been noted (but who, admittedly, lived to see Henry VIII on the throne of England), states categorically that Richard murdered his nephews, and comments that 'he lost his wife; some said he had her killed'. Commines is not claiming to relate facts, but faithfully records opinions commonly held at the time. If Richard had killed Anne, or even wished her dead, in order that he could marry his own niece, he would no doubt have done so regardless of popular opinion. The sole evidence that he considered it is a letter which no longer exists, if it ever did. On the contrary, an embassy was sent to Portugal to attempt to negotiate marriages for both Richard himself and his niece, Elizabeth of York, with members of that royal family. It is reasonable to exonerate him from all blame for the death of Anne Neville, that sad young woman who had been Queen of England for less than two years.

For several centuries, there was no memorial to Anne in Westminster Abbey where she had been buried. The Richard III Society, attributing this omission to her husband's preoccupation with the imminent Tudor invasion, erected one in 1960. Every year, on the anniversary of her death, the society holds a service in her honour. I have never been present at one of these; but it is doubtful whether reference is ever made to the short period when Anne Neville held the title of Princess of Wales.

Katherine of Aragon
(1485–1536)

In 1501 a Spanish ship arrived in Plymouth, carrying a very important passenger. For the first time in its short history, the title of Princess of Wales would be held by a woman who had not been born in the British Isles. Some people may be surprised to hear the name of Katherine of Aragon in connection with the title of Princess of Wales. Her early history is generally forgotten in favour of the later years of her life. She is best known to us as the first of the six wives of Henry VIII, but her time as Princess of Wales, though very brief, is crucial to what happened during her marriage to Henry. It had far-reaching consequences for the whole kingdom, which are still felt today.

Katherine's name is probably the best known of any of the post-Edwardian Princesses of Wales. She gained the title when the Welsh-born King Henry VII of England brought her from Spain to marry his elder son, Arthur. Their marriage was short-lived, but the question of whether it was ever consummated was to be one of the most important issues in the history of England. The Spanish bride is now remembered chiefly as one of the most hard-done-by English queens.

She was born in December 1485, the fourth and youngest daughter of Ferdinand of Aragon and Isabella of Castile, the patrons of Christopher Columbus. It was just a few months since the throne of England had changed hands. Having survived infancy, Katherine made a good choice of bride for the son of King Henry VII. Through her mother, she was actually descended from the first English Prince of Wales, Edward of Caernarfon. Henry Tudor had managed to retain the Crown since his victory at Bosworth, but was nevertheless a weak claimant, craving international approval to help maintain his position. Spain and England shared a common enemy in France, so a

*Katherine of Aragon, Princess of Wales, later the first wife of
King Henry VIII. From a Victorian print.*

marriage alliance made sense. In a sad postscript to the story of Anne Neville (the previous Princess of Wales), the Spanish are alleged to have insisted that Henry remove the leading rival claimant to the throne, Edward, Earl of Warwick, whose supporters had already attempted an uprising. Henry found a pretext in 1499, when the earl made a feeble attempt to escape from prison. He was promptly executed.

With the Spanish ambassador to England, Dr de Puebla, as chief matchmaker, Katherine of Aragon was betrothed to Arthur Tudor in 1497. A very formal correspondence between them (in Latin) survives. The proxy marriage took place at the palace of Tickenhill in Worcestershire in May 1499, Arthur being resident in nearby Ludlow at the time, and thereafter Katherine was officially referred to as Princess of Wales. It was another two years before the princess actually departed for her future home. She arrived in Plymouth in 1501, having sailed from Corunna with a magnificent train of attendants. King Henry and Prince Arthur caught up with them at a village in Berkshire, ostensibly to welcome Katherine to England. Spanish custom did not permit the prince to set eyes on his bride before their wedding day, but the king, concerned that he might be receiving some deformed or otherwise undesirable creature into the family, insisted on seeing her. He was not disappointed; by all accounts she was a beautiful young woman with fair hair that fell below her waist. Contemporary portraits support the idea that she was attractive. Her lack of height suited her future bridegroom, who was severely undersized for his age. King Henry declared himself pleased with her looks and manners, and the English people were equally approving.

Katherine and Arthur were both aged fifteen at the time of their wedding in St Paul's Cathedral, she being nine months his senior. The emblem of the red dragon, adopted by Henry VII after the example of Prince Cadwaladr and now traditionally associated with Wales, was much in evidence during the wedding celebrations at Baynard's Castle. Arthur and Katherine spent their wedding night in the bishop of London's palace near St Paul's. It had been newly decorated, and had the luxury of glass in the windows.

The tradition of public bedding in that period is well attested, and the marriage of Arthur and Katherine was no exception. It

was important that there should be witnesses to the consum-
mation of such a match, but in practice this was mere ceremonial.
Thirty years later, when the future of the English monarchy
depended on it, it was impossible to find anyone who had observed the actual physical union, not only on the wedding night
but at any time during the marriage. The nearest anyone came
to it at the tribunal appointed to inquire into the matter was to
quote Arthur as having said, on the first morning of his married
life, that he had 'been in Spain' during the night. That statement is clearly open to interpretation.

Although the two young people had written to one another
in the common language of Latin, their accents would have
prevented them from speaking it to one another, and Katherine
had yet to learn English. Since they were unable to hold a proper
conversation, it would perhaps have been difficult for them to
achieve intimacy in these early stages of their marriage. Sadly,
there was little time for them to get to know one another.

Arthur's death took place in April 1502 at Ludlow, where he
and Katherine had been sent a few weeks after their marriage, in
order to 'govern' the principality of Wales. Henry Tudor, though
no sentimentalist, had named his eldest son after that legendary
king of ancient Britain whose connection with Wales is traditional. Henry, himself being Welsh-born and of Welsh blood,
had determined that the title of Prince of Wales should cease to
be an honorary one.

Arthur Tudor's council was made up largely of Englishmen
hand-picked by his astute father, but it provided the Welsh with
an identity recognized by the London government. Henry clearly
felt he owed this much to the country where he had been born
and gathered such loyal support (though he never visited it after
becoming king). Noble Welsh families such as the Griffiths,
Vaughans and Herberts came to Ludlow to pay their respects to
Arthur, but it was the nearest the prince and princess ever came
to Wales. A walkway was built at Ludlow Castle, apparently for
the use of Katherine and her ladies-in-waiting. From here they
could see across the border. Visitors to the ruined castle can
still see the rooms set aside for the use of the young prince and
princess. 'Look, Dad, this is King Arthur's bedroom,' children

tell their parents. We will never know what kind of king Arthur Tudor might have made. We know far more about his wife.

It is ironic that the traditional Welsh wet weather probably contributed to the illness that caused Arthur's untimely death. Katherine was simultaneously struck down with the infection, but recovered to find herself a widow, with the title Princess Dowager of Wales. This must have come as a terrible shock to a teenage girl. When she was well enough to leave Ludlow, she was sent to London to live at Durham House, another bishop's residence, and was not brought to court until 1505.

King Ferdinand of Aragon, having foreseen the possibility of Prince Arthur's death, had withheld a large proportion of Katherine's promised dowry. Henry VII, grieving over the death of his elder son, nevertheless had no wish to lose the opportunity of an alliance with Spain. He may even have thought of marrying Katherine himself, when his own wife died the following year. Papal dispensation was required in order to allow his surviving son, Henry, to be betrothed to Katherine. This was granted on the basis that the Princess of Wales had remained a virgin throughout her marriage to Arthur Tudor. In practice, it was a formality. There is no shortage of contemporary examples in similar cases where no such demand was made, regardless of what the Bible may have to say on the subject. Two of Katherine's older sisters had been successively married to the same King of Portugal. The pope had the power to remove any obstacles if he so wished. On the other hand, Katherine and her attendants knew as well as her father-in-law did that, if the marriage had been consummated, she would have been entitled to reclaim her dowry, which would no doubt have suited her family.

Arthur's younger brother was still only twelve, and there was bound to be some delay before any marriage could take place. At the time of their betrothal in 1503, Katherine still held the title of Princess of Wales, whilst her future husband was Duke of York. He was quickly invested with the title Prince of Wales by letters patent, but did not succeed his brother as head of the Council of Wales. No doubt the loss of one son at Ludlow turned Henry VII against the idea of sending his remaining heir to wild wet Wales. Meanwhile, his queen, Elizabeth of York, had died in childbirth, making one last noble attempt to supply him with more heirs. The loss of her mother-in-law left Katherine without a female role model or source of comfort within the royal family.

Despite the steps taken to secure Katherine for Prince Henry, the couple, originally scheduled to marry when the prince reached the age of fifteen, did not actually do so until two months after Henry became king in 1509. Thus Katherine became the second Princess of Wales in succession to achieve the throne of England in the company of a different husband from the Prince of Wales she had started out with. Though nearly six years Katherine's junior, Henry VIII was a better proposition both as a king and as a husband, being in robust health, handsome, talented and popular, a true Renaissance prince. However, he had seemed for a while to be slipping out of her grasp. His father, still quibbling with Spain over the payment of Katherine's dowry, had begun to inquire into the possibility of other suitable marriages for his remaining son, with European princesses such as Eleanor of Austria. Katherine's mother, Isabella, had died, and Ferdinand had entered into a marriage alliance with the French. On the matter of the dowry, he called the English king's bluff.

Prince Henry seems to have been instructed to break off his betrothal to Katherine in 1504, and the Princess Dowager of Wales spent several years of uncertainty, living in isolation and suffering from various illnesses symptomatic of her mental state. Apart from a visit from her sister Juana in 1506, there was little cause for optimism. Her letters to her father make clear her distress. 'I have had so much pain and annoyance,' she wrote, 'that I have lost my health in a great measure, so that for two months I have had severe tertian fevers, and this will be the cause that I shall soon die.'

By the terms of her first marriage, Katherine should have received a third of the revenues of Wales, and also of Chester and Cornwall, but they were never paid to her. All seemed finally resolved when the King of England died, and his heir promptly announced his intention of marrying her after all. The wedding took place at Greenwich within two months of Henry's accession, and the couple were crowned on Midsummer Day 1509, with lavish celebrations. Katherine wore a richly embroidered dress of white satin, and was carried in a litter, whilst her new husband, dressed in crimson velvet, went on horseback.

In the early years of their marriage, Katherine and Henry seem to have been extremely happy. We can imagine how he must have viewed her from a distance, an attractive girl who had achieved sexual maturity but had been kept out of the boy's grasp by his father's whims. At last he was answerable to no one, and could claim what was rightfully his. The young couple clearly had fun in the early years of their marriage. They wrote poems to one another. Henry was very musical, loved dancing and play-acting, and had a great sense of humour. He enjoyed tricks and disguises, turning up at parties in fancy dress. On one occasion, the young king and some of his friends arrived dressed as Robin Hood and his merry men. Katherine was expected to pretend that she did not recognize them!

Things started to go wrong after the loss of their first son at the age of seven weeks, followed by several stillbirths. The only child who survived was a girl, Mary (later to go down in history as 'Bloody Mary'), born at Greenwich in February 1516. Although Henry maintained an outward display of devotion to his queen, he was beginning to look elsewhere. Mistress after mistress undermined the queen's position, some providing bastard sons, but Katherine seems to have remained oblivious to the danger. Her performance as Henry's deputy in times of national emergency strengthened her claim on his affections, and her popularity within the country showed no sign of waning.

Charles V, Katherine's nephew, was duly elected Holy Roman Emperor, and he travelled to England to meet his aunt at Canterbury in 1520. If Henry had ideas of discarding Katherine, he momentarily put them to one side for the sake of political expediency. Shortly after the emperor's visit, the queen accompanied her husband to France, for a meeting with the French king that became known as the Field of the Cloth of Gold. Princess Mary continued to be recognized as the heir to the throne.

In 1526 Katherine became seriously ill, and death seemed a possibility. It seems to have been around this time that she became aware of what was in Henry's mind. She had spies of her own who reported back on the poisonous activities of the king's adviser, Cardinal Wolsey. Wolsey had tried to convince the pope that Katherine was keen to enter a convent. Moreover, the cardinal was colluding with Henry to arrange an ecclesiastical hearing to review the legitimacy of the royal marriage.

Henry had been seized with a desire to replace his middle-aged and now overweight wife with the young and apparently fertile Ann Boleyn, a former attendant of Katherine's, and he used the queen's previous marriage to his brother as grounds for divorce. He may have genuinely believed that the lack of a legitimate heir was God's judgement on him for going against the rulings of scripture, having studied the now notorious text of Leviticus 18:16 and 20:21, both of which appear to forbid a man to marry his brother's widow or ex-wife. Henry assured the council that it was nothing personal, describing her as 'a woman of most gentleness, humility, and buxomness; yea, and of all good qualities pertaining to nobility she is without comparison. So that if I were to marry again, I would choose her above all women.' (The meaning of 'buxomness', in this case, is 'attractiveness'.)

Katherine, even when faced with a public hearing to investigate the incident, denied that she had ever had sexual intercourse with Arthur, Prince of Wales, in the few months they were married. She defied Wolsey when he came to see her to negotiate, refusing to speak to him in private. When he tried to talk to her in Latin, so that those present would not understand, she insisted he speak English. Before the court of inquiry, she remained adamant, and she knelt in front of the king and addressed him directly. Shakespeare paraphrases her speech thus:

> In what have I offended you? What cause
> Hath my behaviour given to your displeasure,
> That thus you should proceed to put me off,
> And take your good grace from me?

Shakespeare's patron was Queen Elizabeth I, the daughter of Ann Boleyn, so he had no reason to show sympathy for Katherine in his play, *King Henry VIII*, but he was reflecting popular feeling.

The truth is forever lost. We may choose to suppose that Katherine, being a devout Roman Catholic, would have found falsehood repugnant. However, having gone through with a marriage to Henry and borne him a child, it would have been equally difficult for her to pronounce herself guilty of fornication and have her only child, her daughter Mary, labelled a bastard – something that would happen in spite of her best efforts.

In 1531 the queen was commanded to leave the royal residence at Windsor for a house in Bedfordshire. There was considerable support for her position: she had retained the popularity originally earned as Princess of Wales. The majority of the clergy were on her side, though they dared not say so; and only a year earlier the female population of Oxford had thrown unpleasant missiles at the official emissaries who came to assess popular opinion on the subject of a royal divorce.

Since Pope Clement VII (heavily influenced by Katherine's nephew, the Holy Roman Emperor) refused to grant Henry his divorce, he obtained it by breaking his allegiance to Rome, creating the basis of the Church of England. In 1533 Henry's marriage to Katherine was annulled by his 'tame' archbishop of Canterbury, Thomas Cranmer. Religious unrest would dominate Britain for the next two hundred years. Following the annulment, a new Act of Succession took away both Katherine's right to be called queen and her daughter's status as heir, whilst imposing an oath of changed allegiance on all male subjects. This proved the undoing of Sir Thomas More, among others. Princess Mary likewise refused to sign away her own legitimacy. Her long-standing governess, the Countess of Salisbury (a daughter of George, Duke of Clarence), took the blame and was dismissed.

Interestingly, although Henry's son, Edward (the product of his third marriage, to Jane Seymour), never officially held the title of Prince of Wales, Edward's two half-sisters, Mary and Elizabeth, were both addressed at various times as either Prince of Wales or Princess of Wales. This was a courtesy title acknowledging their position as Henry's heirs before Edward's birth. There was no formal precedent for recognizing a female child as heir to the throne of England. The only time it had previously been tried, back in the twelfth century, it had resulted in the civil war between King Stephen and his cousin, Matilda.

For a time, Mary had held the official title of governor of Wales, and resided at Ludlow as president of the council, still active after Prince Arthur's death. In 1525 the princess had been given her own household, along with several residences including Ludlow Castle itself and Tickenhill, where the proxy marriage between Katherine and Arthur had taken place. To digress momentarily from Katherine's story, it was Henry VIII, recognizing his Welsh blood and his responsibility towards the principality, who would introduce the Acts of Union by which England and Wales were formally made one. The Acts of 1536 and 1543 gave Wales and England a uniform legal system, gave Wales representation in Parliament, and enabled Welshmen to gain promotion to official posts. One unfortunate effect of this was to weaken the connection between the title of Prince of Wales and the government of the principality.

The same petty actions which resulted in Katherine's being demoted and physically moved, first to Ampthill, then to the bishop of Lincoln's palace at Buckden, and finally to Kimbolton Castle in the east of England, caused her daughter to lose her position in the line of succession. Mary's household was dismissed, and she became little more than a lady-in-waiting to her infant half-sister, Elizabeth, the child of Ann Boleyn.

Katherine, following her divorce, was addressed by the title of dowager Princess of Wales, Henry's way of insisting on her relationship to him as that of sister-in-law, rather than ex-wife. It was not a title that could ever satisfy her, and she continued to sign herself 'Katherine the Queen' in all correspondence. Worn out by resisting her destiny, she died at Kimbolton in 1536, of a form of cancer, only a few months before Henry divorced her successor, Ann Boleyn, in favour of Jane Seymour (who had, like Ann, been one of Katherine's ladies-in-waiting). By this time, Katherine was virtually a prisoner, served only by a handful of loyal women.

Eustace Chapuys, the Spanish ambassador who had befriended the queen in the last years of her marriage, attended Katherine on her deathbed. Chapuys had given Katherine a blow-by-blow account of the marriage difficulties that Ann Boleyn was already experiencing. Her continued hope was that she might one day regain her status as queen. In the last few days of her life, however, she recognized the inevitable and wrote to Henry,

A view from Ludlow Castle – the nearest Katherine of Aragon ever came to Wales. Photo © Rhys Jones, LRPS.

imploring him to see her one last time before she died. 'My Lord and Dear Husband,' she wrote. 'The hour of my death draweth fast on . . . I commend unto you Mary, our daughter, be-seeching you to be a good father unto her, as I heretofore desired . . . Lastly, I do vow, that mine eyes desire you above all things.'

There was no hope of the request being fulfilled; Katherine was not even allowed to see her daughter. She was buried, not in St Paul's as would have been fitting for a queen, but in Peterborough Cathedral (in a spot nowadays marked by an iron grille bearing the words 'Katharine the Queen' and often decorated with flowers), with only the degree of ceremony due to a one-time Princess of Wales. Officiating at the funeral, the bishop of Rochester took the opportunity of preaching a sermon on the royal supremacy. The king did not attend, and Princess Mary was forbidden to pay her last respects in person. Katherine's replacement as queen, Ann Boleyn, in a spiteful action which reveals her darker side, commanded her ladies-in-waiting to wear yellow to celebrate the demise of the dowager Princess of Wales. With Katherine's death, Ann must have thought her troubles were at an end.

In 1534, Katherine had written to her daughter, from the prison-like residence to which she had been banished, attempting to offer hope for the future: 'I dare make sure that you shall see a very good end, and better than you can desire . . . we never come to the kingdom of Heaven but by troubles.' This was prophetic; in less than twenty years, Mary herself would sit on the throne. Yet Katherine of Aragon's farewell message draws a line under her tenure as princess and queen. Two hundred years would pass between the Spanish bride and the next woman to hold the title of Princess of Wales. Like Katherine, she would be foreign born.

Caroline of Ansbach (1683–1737)

In the two centuries since the death of Katherine of Aragon, Britain had changed. A succession of events, resulting indirectly from Henry VIII's callous treatment of Katherine, threatened the stability of the monarchy. After the Reformation, religious upheaval continued through the reigns of Henry's children. Edward VI followed an extreme Protestant line, but Mary Tudor tried to reintroduce the Roman model of Catholicism. Finally came Elizabeth I, who returned the country to a more moderate track. Elizabeth died unmarried, and the throne of England went to her closest relative, the King of Scotland. Under the Stuarts, mainland Britain became a single, 'united' kingdom, but religion still caused problems. Charles I's Catholic leanings helped start a civil war; unfortunately, it did not end there. Charles II, having been restored to the throne and reigned successfully for twenty-five years, also died childless, and his younger brother became King James II.

James was a Roman Catholic, but his first wife had been Protestant, so his daughters, Mary and Anne, were brought up Protestant. When his Catholic second wife gave birth to a son and potential heir, another popular revolution (the Glorious or Bloodless Revolution) removed James and put his daughters on the throne. Like the Tudor queens, they both died without heirs, and by 1714 the country was back to square one, looking for a replacement among their Protestant relatives in Germany; hence the beginnings of the Hanoverian dynasty.

The next woman officially to bear the title of Princess of Wales was a German-born princess, Caroline, daughter of the margrave of Brandenburg-Ansbach. Caroline's husband, George Augustus, became Prince of Wales when his father George I

Caroline of Ansbach, wife of King George II.
From a Victorian print.

was invited to take the throne of England on the death of
Queen Anne in 1714, becoming the first in the Hanoverian or
'Georgian' line. The prince had already been married for several
years.

Caroline was a woman of character, intelligent as well as
beautiful. Born in March 1683, she had not had the easiest childhood. Her father died when she was four, and she was brought
up by her mother and her stepfather, the elector of Saxony.
Before she was old enough to marry, her stepfather died, closely
followed by her mother. The philosopher Leibniz, a friend of

Caroline's guardian, was often the source of spiritual guidance in later years. Despite her orphaned state, she was much sought after as a bride. After failing to catch the Duke of Saxe-Gotha (whose daughter would later become Caroline's daughter-in-law), she had the opportunity of becoming Queen of Spain. The marriage would have required her to convert to Roman Catholicism; she refused. Her time would soon come. When she met Prince George, heir to the tiny state of Hanover, he was immediately smitten.

In September 1714, shortly after the couple's arrival on British shores, George was invested with the title of Prince of Wales at Westminster, and the honeymoon really began. Caroline of Ansbach was thirty-one at the time she became Princess of Wales, and is worthy of note for being the first to succeed in achieving the status of queen without upset. Perhaps it would be more accurate to say 'without *much* upset'. The prince had a very stormy relationship with his father, the king. Nevertheless, the title of Prince of Wales was conferred on him immediately, in what was no doubt a political gesture.

There is a popular misconception that women of the eighteenth century had little influence on public life or politics. This ignores a tradition of active political involvement on the part of noblewomen who were not deterred from participating by the fact that they had no vote (and would not have one for another two hundred years). Although her ability to participate actively in politics may have been constrained by her royal title, Caroline of Ansbach was definitely one such woman.

To those familiar with her life and habits, Caroline comes across as a modern woman, with a comparable outlook to the one which others of her gender have today. By the time she assumed the title of Princess of Wales in 1714, women's lives were not dictated by their husbands' occupations to the extent they had once been; they had minds of their own and knew what they wanted out of life. It was easier for women in general to obtain an education than it had been two hundred years before. Life for a princess still meant putting duty and husband before her own wishes, but the role of the Princess of Wales was going to be a more distinctive one than it had been before, partly because of an almost continuous line of Princesses of Wales leading right up to the end of the twentieth century.

The explanation is a reduction in early and violent death, giving Princes of Wales time to marry. There had not been an adult Prince of Wales since Charles II, who had never officially been invested with the title, so it was something of a novelty for the British people when a new one arrived on their shores – not least for the Welsh, who basked in the temporary limelight.

In 1694, when their son was eleven, George I had divorced his wife for adultery. Sophia Dorothea remained shut away in the Castle of Ahlden in Germany until her death in 1726, and he loathed her memory. The arrival of the Princess of Wales was especially welcome because there was no queen, George never having remarried. However, the days when the heir to the throne had been trained for his future responsibilities by being sent to govern Wales were long past; the monarchy had been effectively rendered powerless following the overthrow of Charles I and James II. Caroline would nevertheless make the most of her opportunities to become the 'power behind the throne', if there was one.

Before the end of the Hanoverian royal line, family strife would be the order of the day. L. G. Pine lays several accusations on the Hanoverian kings, not least their failure to prepare their sons adequately. Pine notes three distinctive characteristics of the Hanoverian line: firstly, the mutual hostility between father and eldest son which recurred in all but one case; secondly, the king's refusal to allow the heir an adequate political education; and, finally, the lack of morality in their private lives. 'The education of a Prince of Wales right up to the Hanoverian succession was automatically understood to include a deliberate understudying of his father's position,' notes Pine. Whether the change can be attributed to the new line of kings as individuals or whether it has more to do with the political climate in which they were operating is debatable.

From the thirteenth century, when the title Prince of Wales was conferred on the eldest son of the King of England, it had been recognized that it carried with it the responsibility of acting as a kind of deputy to the monarch, and being prepared to take on the kingship when the time came. Under the Hanoverians, this was ceasing to be the case. Monarchs were increasingly reluctant to share the reins of power with their sons, and the Prince of Wales, besides having no obvious connection with his principality, no longer had any obvious role. This becomes more apparent in the way that George II later refused to let his son, Frederick, have any part in government.

The Welsh were delighted to learn that the birthday of their new princess fell on 1st March, St David's Day. Compared with the rest of her family, Caroline was a cultured person, an art collector and an excellent dancer. A group of Welshmen resident in London formed a patriotic society of which the Prince of Wales agreed to become president, despite having little interest in the principality beyond the revenues it provided. Every year, on Caroline's birthday, the London Welsh celebrated with a Welsh sermon in a London church, followed by a banquet at which favours of silver ribbon bearing the motto 'Caroline and St David' were worn. We begin to see parallels with the more recent attention paid to a non-Welsh Princess of Wales.

The eldest son of the Prince and Princess of Wales, Frederick Lewis, had been born in 1707 in Hanover, and was left there, at his grandfather's insistence, to finish his schooling when his parents came to England. An ugly, unhealthy child, Frederick was nicknamed the 'Griffin' by his parents. That they could have shown such unkindness to a small child did not bode well for the future, and they would receive repayment in full. Whether his mother knew it or not, the circumstances of Frederick's birth and his general appearance had caused rumours to circulate in Hanover about his true paternity. (Tellingly, George referred to his son as a Wechselbald, translating this, for the benefit of his listeners, as 'a child put in a cradle instead of another'.) Frederick, meanwhile, retained the nickname of 'Griff' for the rest of his life.

It is difficult for a modern parent to comprehend what would make a mother develop such an antipathy towards her first-born child as Caroline of Ansbach did. We would be tempted to point to post-natal depression or some other psychological cause for her subsequent conduct towards him. In point of fact, having been separated from Frederick before he reached his eighth birthday, it is not entirely surprising if she transferred her affection for him to her other children, those who accompanied her on the journey to a new home in Britain. The adulation heaped on George and Caroline must have diverted them from any lingering thoughts of their eldest son, across the sea in Germany.

There were, by then, several other children, all girls. Anne, named in honour of the British queen, had been born in 1709, Amelia (known as Emily) in 1711, and Caroline in 1713. Not until after their arrival in Britain would Caroline of Ansbach give birth to a second son. Soon his siblings, undoubtedly influenced by their parents, came to dislike Frederick too. 'He was the greatest liar that ever spoke and will put one arm round anybody's neck to kiss them, and then stab them with the other if he can,' declared his sister, Anne.

Before Frederick joined his parents in England in 1728, he had received a Welsh title, that of Baron Snowdon. It is doubtful whether it meant any more to him than the title of Prince of Wales meant to his father. Willingness to grant titles was never, under the Hanoverians, an indication of parental affection. George had little choice in whether to give his son the customary titles (just as his own father had little choice about making him Prince of Wales). By this stage, Queen Caroline seems positively to have hated her own son, whom she called 'the greatest ass, and the greatest liar . . . and the greatest beast in the whole world, and I heartily wish he was out of it'.

How could this bad feeling have started? Without ignoring the outside chance that Frederick may have been illegitimate, his relationship with his parents definitely suffered as a result of the marriage plans he began to make as soon as he was old enough. It had been arranged that he would marry his cousin, Princess Wilhelmina of Prussia, but, for whatever reason, the new King of Great Britain decided against it. Frederick was keen to go ahead with the marriage, and tried in vain to make things happen before he left Hanover.

When the initial threat posed by the first Jacobite rebellion in 1715 was deemed to be over, George I decided it was time to pay a visit to Hanover. Here is the first outright evidence of the antipathy between father and son which would be passed down through the generations. The king had no choice but to allow his son, the Prince of Wales, to act as his deputy in his absence, but took pleasure in denying him the title of regent, choosing instead to call him 'Guardian of the Realm', a title carrying less extensive powers and privileges.

Further children soon came along to create an additional distraction. A stillbirth, a miscarriage and the loss of a son at three months of age were severe blows to the couple's happiness, but a further three children were safely born in the years up to 1724. When Caroline gave birth to her second son, George, in 1717, there was a family quarrel at the christening, because the king had invited the Duke of Newcastle to be a godfather without consulting the parents. The disagreement resulted in the Prince of Wales being placed in detention and the couple being evicted from their official residence in St James's Palace. They were forced to leave behind their youngest children, including the baby prince. The boy died at the age of four months, and accusations of neglect flew around.

The prince and princess moved into a private house in Leicester Square, where they set up a kind of rival court, attracting members of the political opposition. The last three of their nine children were born there. It was Caroline, through her friendship with the prime minister, Robert Walpole, who managed to re-establish friendly terms with the king, at least sporadically, and there was a formal reconciliation in 1720. Walpole ensured that the Prince and Princess of Wales continued to be financially provided for. In spite of this rapprochement, the king saw Caroline as a threat to any vain hope he might have had of bringing his son to heel, referring to her on one occasion as 'a devil'.

Every so often, the Prince of Wales held a levee. Those in favour at the alternative court were invited to come and watch the prince getting up and getting dressed: putting on his outer garments, that is. This was a formal, ceremonial occasion, and those in the royal presence were not allowed to sit. Although the king had little to do with his son, he liked to hear what was going on behind the scenes at the prince's house. There was one salacious little story, about how one of Princess Caroline's ladies-in-waiting was desperate to go to the toilet on one of these occasions. Forbidden to leave the princess's side, she relieved herself where she stood, making a sizeable puddle.

Later the Prince and Princess of Wales lived at Richmond Park. There, George built a Palladian villa, known as the White Lodge. It would one day be the childhood home of another Princess of Wales and the birthplace of a Prince of Wales (Mary of Teck and her eldest son, David). George and Caroline were together in bed one night when Walpole arrived at Richmond with the news that the prince's father had died during a visit to Hanover, and they were now king and queen. It was news the prince found difficult to believe. He is alleged to have responded, in his imperfect English: 'Dat is vun beeg lie!'

After the king's death, Caroline went through his papers, and discovered just how far out of favour her husband had fallen. Among the late king's effects, she found a proposal from a royal adviser to transport the Prince of Wales to America, still a British colony. She can hardly have been sorry to see the back of her father-in-law. George I had not been universally popular with his subjects, either. There were scenes of mass adulation when George and Caroline returned to London to take their place as king and queen. Walpole's past generosity towards the couple ensured his political survival.

Caroline was a big success as queen. She was a mature woman, forty-four years old, and she undoubtedly 'wore the trousers' in this marriage. More intelligent than her husband, she chose to tolerate his frequent infidelities. She even allowed him to confide in her about his mistresses, recognizing that he was dependent on her for companionship, for advice, and as a means of maintaining his popularity. She had the talent that he lacked, for dealing with people, and enjoyed flirting as much as he did.

Caroline had a civilized arrangement with Lady Suffolk, her husband's favourite mistress for many years. To be on the safe side, she ensured that Lady Suffolk's influence was limited to the bedroom by preventing any of the Suffolk family from achieving positions of political influence. When Lady Suffolk fell out with the king in 1735, Caroline was not altogether happy; she did not look forward to a newcomer who might try to undermine her influence over her husband.

Although newspapers were in their infancy, satire, in the form of pamphlets and popular songs, was widespread, and the royal family did not escape criticism. The relationship between the king and queen was summed up in a popular rhyme:

You may strut, dapper George, but 'twill all be in vain;
We know 'tis Queen Caroline, not you, that reign.

Both Caroline and the king disliked their eldest son. They preferred his younger brother, William, Duke of Cumberland, later
to be the victor at Culloden and now remembered chiefly, as
'Butcher' Cumberland for his brutal treatment of the Highlanders.
(Frederick had been rejected as a military commander.) It is
even alleged that George II considered a scheme for sending
Frederick to rule Hanover so that William could succeed his
father on the British throne. At Hampton Court, his parents'
main residence, a set of apartments was built in 1732 for the
young duke. The Cumberland Suite was designed by William
Kent and built at a cost of £3,454. The king and queen were prepared to be as generous to their younger son as they were stingy
towards the heir to the throne.

The worsening situation between the royal couple and their
eldest son was inflamed by courtiers like Lord Hervey, who had
fallen out with the Prince of Wales over a woman. As a friend,
Hervey was no great loss to Frederick, who proceeded to surround
himself with artists and musicians and whose favourite com-
panions included the elder Pitt and the author Tobias Smollett.
The prince's hobbies included art, astronomy, botany, music,
science and the theatre.

Hervey's Ciceronian phrases listing Frederick's many faults
were composed largely at the instigation of the queen. Furthermore, despite holding the office of vice-chamberlain to King
George II, Hervey was almost equally condemnatory about his
royal master. Of Caroline herself, he remarked that 'her will
was the sole spring on which every movement in the Court
turned, and though His Majesty lost no opportunity to declare
that the Queen never meddled with his business, yet nobody
was simple enough to believe it'.

Although Frederick now held the title Prince of Wales, the king
continued to keep back half the income from the principality.
The prince's expenditure was prodigal, and he had fallen into
debt. In 1732 he had a royal barge built by William Kent, which
can now be seen in the Maritime Museum at Greenwich. As
with so many of his actions, this was in part a spiteful gesture
against his parents. In politics, knowing his mother to be a friend

of the prime minister, Frederick sided with the opposition. His father was a patron of Handel, so Frederick patronized rival composers, such as Porpora. The prince was particularly hurt by the fact that his father continued to overlook his position as heir to the throne. When George II went abroad for an extended period, as he did several times in the 1720s and 1730s, it was Caroline he always left with the powers of regent. History was repeating itself.

In 1735 the Prince of Wales published a book, which he may or may not have written himself. The strangely titled *Histoire du Prince Titi* cruelly satirized both his parents. That was the end of any lingering hopes of reconciliation. Eventually, Frederick went to his father and demanded an increase in his allowance and a suitable wife, which he hoped would bring in extra funds. The king, his patience exhausted, agreed, on condition that Frederick show proper respect to his mother in the future. We can only imagine what had been going on between mother and son in private.

The king and queen began to look around for someone with the right pedigree. They were not concerned with the happiness of the son who had given them so much grief; they merely wanted to shut him up. As for Frederick, he was eager for marriage simply because it guaranteed an increase in his living allowance. Parliament had set aside £100,000 a year for the Prince of Wales; he was receiving half that amount, out of the Civil List. In terms of a choice of bride for Frederick, Caroline was looking for someone who would not threaten to steal the limelight. Now that she was getting older, the last thing she wanted was another woman to share her popularity. Even as Princess of Wales, she had been the first lady in the land.

Frederick and his bride, Augusta, were obliged to spend their first few months of married life at St James's Palace, under the eyes of the king and queen, where no doubt it was expected that their actions could be kept under control. This was quite normal for a royal couple, and would continue to be so well into the twentieth century. At first it seemed that things were going according to plan, but the new princess started to show that she had a mind of her own (or at any rate that her first loyalty would be to her husband), and Caroline soon became jealous.

The increase in his financial allowance, welcome as it may have been, was not enough for Frederick. He was able to recognize sympathizers in the House of Commons. William Pitt spoke ironically of the joy felt by the king on the happy occasion of his son's marriage, and lost preferment as a result of his rudeness. He was celebrated by the opposition, who now took up the cause of the Prince of Wales and his financial necessity. In 1737, they successfully moved to have the prince's allowance raised to the £100,000 to which he was entitled in the terms of the Civil List.

His parents never forgave him. Unconcerned with their good opinion, Frederick continued to spend lavishly. After his marriage, he entertained a thousand guests to a banquet at Carlton House. It made the young couple very popular. Pitt would later be rewarded with a position as groom of the bedchamber.

The Princess of Wales, thought observers at Hampton Court in the summer of 1737, was too slim to be nine months pregnant. Queen Caroline, who may by this time have been aware that she had only a short time to live, expressed doubts about the genuineness of her daughter-in-law's pregnancy. Apparently this was because she did not believe her son capable of fathering a child, not because she believed Augusta to have had relations with anyone other than Frederick. Doubts about his virility remained in spite of the existence of two illegitimate sons; it was rumoured that one of these had been fathered by Lord Hervey.

Disbelieving in the pregnancy, and in a repeat of her own father-in-law's conduct towards herself, Caroline tried to ensure that she was present at the birth, and allegedly told Hervey: 'At her labour I positively will be, let her lie-in where she will; for she cannot be brought to bed as quick as one can blow one's nose and I will be sure it is her child.'

The prince thwarted her by having his wife moved from Hampton Court to St James's Palace in the middle of her labour, without his parents' knowledge. They did not catch up with events until the following day. The king was furious over the deception. On seeing the child, however, it seems that Caroline's maternal instincts reasserted themselves. When she arrived at St James's (probably spoiling for a fight), she kissed the baby, saying: 'The Good Lord bless you, you poor little creature. You have arrived in a very disagreeable world.'

We may choose to excuse some of Caroline's earlier behaviour on the grounds that she was already in the painful grip of her fatal illness; but two months before she died, her son and daughter-in-law were given notice to leave the royal residence because the king was not satisfied with the apology he had received for the incident just described. Repeating history, the king evicted the prince and princess, along with their young child, from their royal apartments, ordering his son to leave 'as soon as ever the safety and convenience of the Princess will permit'. Copies of his letter to the prince were sent to British embassies abroad and to foreign ambassadors in London. They were actively discouraged from making any future visits to the Prince of Wales and his family.

The prince's situation was not desperate, as he had property of his own, as well as a villa at Kew, which he leased from the Earl of Essex. The young parents began by moving into Carlton House, which they also owned. Those within the royal circle were, however, warned that anyone who paid court to the Prince and Princess of Wales would not thereafter be received by the king and queen.

Caroline of Ansbach died of complications following a ruptured womb, at St James's Palace in 1737, still shunning her eldest son. Her reported deathbed words were 'At least I shall have one comfort in having my eyes eternally closed – I shall never see that monster again.' Her death removed one of the major obstacles to an improved relationship between Frederick and his father.

Visitors to Hampton Court Palace can still tour Queen Caroline's private apartments, which she used from 1727 until her death ten years later. On display in the 'Georgian Rooms' (which include the splendid apartments designed by William Kent for that favoured younger son, the Duke of Cumberland) are some of Caroline's personal effects. We can see where she slept, washed and dressed. Exhibited in her private drawing room are other items which she used in her leisure time, including a card table – perhaps the very one at which she and her husband were playing quadrille when Frederick and his wife left the palace by the back stairs for St James's.

Caroline's passing was greatly mourned by her husband, who stated that he had never met another woman 'fit to buckle her shoe'. When, on her deathbed, she urged him to remarry, he is alleged to have replied tearfully: 'Non, non, j'aurai des maîtresses' ('No, no, I will have mistresses').

No change there, then. Yet George does seem to have retained a strange devotion to Caroline throughout their married life. He had already arranged for his wife and himself to be buried in a pair of matching coffins at Westminster Abbey. The coffins were designed with a removable side, so that after death their dust could mingle and they might continue to be as close in death as they had been in life. The king lived another twenty-three years.

Augusta of Saxe-Gotha
(1719–1772)

Augusta of Saxe-Gotha was one of only three Princesses of Wales who never became queen, and is undoubtedly the least known. In her failure to reach the throne, Augusta stands in good company, midway between the beautiful, popular Joan of Kent and the beautiful, popular Diana Spencer. Augusta herself was not beautiful, and suffered great unpopularity after her son's accession to the throne. Hers was not a long life, and, like all the other holders of the title, she knew great unhappiness and physical suffering as well as enjoying periods of fulfilment and contentment.

On further investigation, there is ample reason for Augusta to be remembered. Although never queen, she was the mother of the longest-reigning king of Britain, over whose early life she exercised great influence. Towards the end of her life and afterwards, the princess was reviled, owing to a widespread belief that her son, George III, was under her thumb and that of his tutor, with whom Augusta was alleged to be having an affair. She became a convenient scapegoat for the country's ills. Today, historians question the extent of the role she played in politics, concluding that she was always on the sidelines and committed none of the indiscretions of which contemporaries accused her. Guilty or not, hers was a notable life, lived at the centre of events which would change the course of British history.

Looking back over a period of almost three hundred years to Augusta's birth, it is hard to imagine life without the mass media. In 1750, a journey from Edinburgh to London by coach took a minimum of ten days. (John Somervell's coach and 'six stout horses' claimed to take ten days in summer and twelve in winter to do the 400-mile trip.) *The London Journal* was regarded as the fount of all knowledge by residents of cities other than the capital.

Augusta of Saxe-Gotha, wife of Frederick, Prince of Wales, and mother of King George III. From a Victorian print.

The Times would not commence publication until 1785. It contained drawings, or 'cartoons' as we know them, in place of photographs. Its 'news' was several days old.

Imagine the feelings of a seventeen-year-old girl, speaking only German and a little French, on being taken from the bosom of her family and told that she is about to become Princess of Wales. If Augusta had ever heard of Wales, she could not have recognized the significance of the title. She would, however, have been informed that this honour carried with it the responsibility of becoming a future Queen of England. Nothing in her early life had prepared her for such a sudden elevation.

Augusta of Saxe-Gotha was born in November 1719, at Gotha in present-day Germany, to Frederick II, Duke of Saxe-Gotha-Altenburg, and his wife, Magdalena Augusta. In 1736, aged seventeen, Augusta was selected as the bride for the heir to the British throne. Frederick was twenty-nine and had been Prince of Wales for seven years. Augusta was closer in age to his younger brother, the Duke of Cumberland. In contrast to her predecessor, Caroline of Ansbach, Augusta had little formal education. She had received a sheltered upbringing, and spoke no English. This was not such a handicap, since few of the Hanoverians had spoken English before arriving in the country, and the first two Georges never achieved a good command of the language.

Frederick, Prince of Wales, may have been one of the most eligible men in Europe, but this had little to do with his personality. Before his arrival in Britain, he had been initiated into adult life by a courtesan who had formerly been mistress not only to his father but also to his grandfather! By the time some attempt at improvement was made, he had developed undisciplined and immoral habits that did not sit well in English society. He was, however, talented and artistic, and his easy manner enabled him to build up a degree of popularity that his parents envied. No wonder they longed for him to settle down to married life.

Augusta was described by her new mother-in-law as 'far from beautiful'. Perhaps this was one reason for favouring her as a daughter-in-law; she would be no rival. The queen's other comments on the girl's appearance were slightly less uncomplimentary: 'She has a wretched figure, pretty eyes and a good mouth. She is anxious as a good child to please. Her hair is almost the same shade as the Duchess of Devonshire's but rather more of a sheep's colour.'

The portrait of Augusta that hangs in Hampton Court Palace, alongside that of her mother-in-law, confirms that she was no rival to Caroline in terms of looks. However, the conventional idea of beauty has changed to such an extent that Caroline herself, with the square-jawed look common to most official portraits of the period, does not immediately captivate the viewer. Neither woman would be considered beautiful by modern standards, but Caroline has an ease and grace about her, whereas Augusta looks rather stiff and not very happy.

Shortly before Augusta's arrival in Britain in April 1736, two unhappy events had occurred in Frederick's life. His mistress, Ann Vane, and their illegitimate child, FitzFrederick, died within a month of one another. This circumstance, of which history has made little, may have predisposed him to welcome his new bride more warmly and with better intentions than other princes of his line.

The new princess, naive and gauche, is said to have arrived at Greenwich carrying a doll, and fell over while attempting to curtsey to the king. Given little time to prepare herself for life as a member of the royal family, with the wedding due to take place a few days later, she was overcome by nausea during the service. Yet her girlish charm only added to her husband's popularity. The couple were married in the Chapel Royal at St James's Palace. On this event, the prince was finally granted an increased allowance of £50,000 a year from Wales, as opposed to the £38,000 he had been receiving as a bachelor.

Lord Hervey's memoirs contain a few spiteful gibes about the wedding ceremony and reception. He describes the prince 'laughing and winking at some of the servants'. Such behaviour by a groom in this day and age would hardly be considered out of place. We would, however, be surprised if the bride and groom were obliged to go to bed together in public, as was still the practice for a royal couple at that time. Queen Caroline supervised the preparations, and the prince entered the bedroom wearing a nightcap which, according to Hervey, 'was some inches higher than any grenadier's cap in the whole army'. The following day, Hervey alleges, he and the queen discussed the wedding night, remarking that the bride looked so refreshed the next morning that she must have slept soundly!

The king and queen could hardly show their disdain for their son in public, and had to put on a show of celebrating his marriage, for form's sake. The wedding saw the first performance of a new anthem, 'Sing unto God', by Handel, the king's favourite composer. In recognition of the momentous event, Handel was also commissioned to produce an opera, *Atalanta*; it contains the aria, *Care selve*, sung by Meleager as he woos the princess of Arcadia. These works were almost guaranteed not to please the Prince of Wales, a sponsor of Handel's leading rivals.

As described in the previous chapter, Queen Caroline was suspicious when Augusta quickly became pregnant, and planned to supervise the birth just as she had supervised the conception. The king and queen were playing cards when the princess felt the first labour pains. Seeing that his parents were preoccupied, and determined that they should not be present at the birth, Frederick hurried his wife down the back stairs. When her waters broke, Augusta pleaded to be left where she was. The prince, without a qualm, insisted on moving her. He is supposed to have rebuked her with the words: 'What nonsense! It will soon be over.'

It was not the norm for expectant fathers to take an interest in their wives' pregnancies, except insofar as these represented evidence of their own potency. Frederick's behaviour, callous as it may seem, may have resulted from an awareness of Augusta's youth and inexperience. No doubt he thought he knew more than she did about everything. In the middle of the night, their carriage rattled back into London. At St James's Palace, their arrival created havoc. Tablecloths had to be used for bedding, as the servants were not expecting them. With the royal couple was Lady Archibald Hamilton, rumoured to have succeeded Ann Vane as the prince's mistress. Lady Archibald's own experience of motherhood was called upon to assist with the delivery, which occurred within the hour.

The Lord Privy Seal, Lord President of the Council and archbishop of Canterbury were woken and witnessed the birth. This precaution, to avoid any future accusation of trickery, demonstrated that Frederick's concern had not been to deceive his mother about the child's parentage, merely to spite her. The outcome was that the couple's first child, Augusta, was born on 12 August 1737, at St James's Palace. She was extremely small. Hervey describes her as 'a little rat of a girl'.

Repeating history, the king evicted the prince and princess from their royal apartments. A rich friend, George Bubb Dodington, had lent Frederick enough to buy Carlton House in Pall Mall, but the upkeep soon proved expensive. Frederick, his resources stretched, decided to lease Norfolk House, in St James's Square, from the Duke of Norfolk. The prince and princess's eldest son – later King George III – was born, once again prematurely, at Norfolk House, where the elderly dowager Duchess of Marlborough, formerly Sarah Churchill, was one of the family's first visitors. The duchess had known Frederick for some years, and he had at one time planned to marry her granddaughter.

Shortly afterwards, Caroline died. Augusta now had to get used to being the most important woman in Britain. Unlike Caroline, she had never sought the limelight, but her husband was the heir to the throne, and one day she expected to be queen. Her position as Princess of Wales could hardly have been more significant. At the same time, she was pregnant again.

The birth occurred in the early morning of 4 June 1738. Lord Egmont's diary says: 'The Princess of Wales was brought to bed of a boy, which the same night received private baptism, there being a doubt if he would live. His Majesty took little notice of it, . . . only laughed and said the sadler's wife was brought to bed . . .' There is no obvious sign, in the king's reaction (with its oblique reference to Frederick's position as governor of the Saddler's Company), of animosity towards his daughter-in-law, otherwise he might have found something more insulting to say.

Frederick was not disposed to forgive his father for real or imagined slights. Not until 1742 was there a formal reconciliation with the king. This occurred after a political upheaval, when the perennial Robert Walpole was toppled from his prime ministerial position, largely as a result of Frederick's support for the opposition. The prince had refused to accept an increased allowance from his father in return for switching allegiance. (Perversely, he would change sides in 1746, following the Jacobite episode.)

The Prince and Princess of Wales moved into Leicester House, a mansion in what is now Leicester Square. The citizens of London gave them a reception. Crowds cheered as their extravagant barge went down the Thames to Greenwich. This was the height of Frederick's popularity, never again equalled. The prince and princess were already spending much of their time at Cliveden, ten miles from Windsor, where the first performance of the song 'Rule Britannia' took place in 1740 as part of a masque held in the amphitheatre. Frederick and Augusta, renting Cliveden from the Countess of Orkney, built up their very own 'Cliveden Set'.

More children were born, mostly at the couple's official London residence. Altogether, Frederick and Augusta had five sons and four daughters. Remarkably, all survived at least into their teens. The evidence suggests that the prince came into his own as a family man. The children were educated at home, and were encouraged to participate in the kind of activities that interested their father, such as amateur theatricals.

Frederick had a rival for the title of Prince of Wales – ironically, Prince Charles Edward Stuart had spent even less of his life in Britain than Frederick had. Bonnie Prince Charlie arrived in Scotland in 1745, to try and recapture the throne of his grandfather, James II. With his younger brother commanding the army, the Prince of Wales expressed no interest in the campaign. While Charlie was besieging Carlisle, Frederick ordered an iced cake, a replica of Carlisle Castle, at which he and his dinner guests threw sugar plums. When the conflict was over, he made a plea for clemency towards the captured rebels, including Flora Macdonald, who had helped Charlie escape to the Continent. Augusta was unsympathetic, expressing the view that Flora Macdonald deserved to be in prison. The prince is said to have replied: 'I hope if I had been in Charles Edward's plight, you would have behaved as Flora Macdonald.' Devoted to her husband Augusta may have been, but heroism was not in her make-up. She had been brought up to put duty before everything else, and she loved her husband and children in the most dutiful way. She would not have dreamed of giving way to her romantic side or of rebelling against authority.

The Prince of Wales's political activities stemmed from a genuine belief that he knew better than his ageing father. There is no evidence whatsoever that he considered his wife capable of understanding current affairs, except insofar as she was capable of obeying his advice and adopting his opinions. As 'king to come', the prince was sure of maintaining some kind of political following. The Leicester House Set were not alone in currying favour. On the other side of the Atlantic, British colonists were advancing inexorably westwards from Pennsylvania and Maryland, into Virginia. Their settlements had become so numerous by 1738 that a portion of the region west of the Blue Ridge Mountains was divided into two counties: Frederick and Augusta. Augusta comprised the southern part of the valley, with Staunton as its county-seat. Already in existence was the city of Augusta, Georgia, named in 1736, the year of the royal wedding.

Frederick was never to become king. He died suddenly in 1751, a fate that had often been publicly wished on him by his mother. His death was brought about by a freak accident. A lively, talented man, his favourite pastimes included cricket and tennis (neither game bore much resemblance to its present form). He was hit by a ball, resulting in an abscess, which burst. Pleurisy or pneumonia aggravated his condition. At the time of his death, one of his household attendants was playing the violin at his bedside to try and cheer him up! As befitted a man who loved music, Frederick's death was marked by the cancellation of the oratorio season. His father, who remained hostile, did not attend the funeral. By a supreme irony, the Prince of Wales was buried in Westminster Abbey, near his hated mother's grave.

His widow, still Britain's first lady, assumed the title of dowager Princess of Wales. Augusta, married to Frederick for only fourteen years, was expecting another child, a girl born nearly four months after his death. Though the king attempted to show kindness to the princess after her bereavement, Frederick's influence was still felt. Augusta despised George, telling Dodington, one of those on whom she now relied, that 'she reckoned the King no more than one of the trees we walked by', and compared him to her youngest son, Henry, in terms of maturity.

One of her first actions on becoming a widow had been to write a courtesy letter to her father-in-law in the most effusive terms. 'The sorrow which overwhelms me,' she wrote, 'does not make me the less sensible of Your Majesty's great goodness.' Clearly this was pure hypocrisy (or diplomacy), as the king no doubt realized. Augusta was aware how dependent she was on his goodwill for her own and her family's welfare. Later, her attitude would harden. Perhaps it dawned on her that, as the mother of the heir apparent, she too had power.

Though she lacked the presence of her predecessor as Princess of Wales, Augusta had character enough to prevent her eldest son, who inherited the title of Prince of Wales at the age of twelve, from living at court under his widowed grandfather's influence. As Princess of Wales, Augusta had played little part in public affairs; now, aged only thirty-two, she came into her own. In return for a degree of compliance, the princess was appointed regent under an Act of Parliament designed to ensure stability of government in the event of the king's dying before his grandson had reached his majority. The selection of the dowager Princess of Wales was probably urged on George by his prime minister, Henry Pelham, in view of the almost universal unpopularity of her main rival, the Duke of Cumberland. Had she been called upon to fulfil this role, she would have been required to take advice from a council led by her hated brother-in-law. It is hard to imagine how the princess would have coped if this unhappy state of affairs had ever come to pass. Uninterested as Augusta claimed to be in politics, would she have accepted the advice offered to her, or might she have been tempted to go her own way?

Almost as though he had foreseen his own death, Frederick had left a document addressed to his son, containing 'instructions' as to how the young man should conduct himself when his turn came to reign. Frederick was far-sighted enough to have recognized the wisdom of a step that would not be taken for many years to come: the breaking of the link between the British Crown and the government of Hanover. This action had been recommended by George I and ignored by George II, which was doubtless what made Frederick so keen on the idea.

It is hard to envisage circumstances in which Augusta would willingly have turned to her husband's family for help. In conversation with Dodington, she referred to Cumberland as her 'great fat friend'. She retained the affection and support of her children, the two eldest sons continuing to live next door in Savile House while she remained at Leicester House. They still had their country residence at Kew. The dowager Princess of Wales continued to resent her father-in-law, and to do everything in her power to thwart him. This tactic meant that her son grew up very isolated. Earl Waldegrave described him as 'full of prejudices which were fostered by women and pages'.

The king had been ready to give the prince a more active role than he had ever willingly offered Frederick. Only a month after the death of the Prince of Wales, a new one was created. Young George simultaneously acquired the title of Earl of Chester, but not the Duchy of Cornwall, which had passed to the Crown. The king was happy to retain the revenues from that rich source; as a result, Augusta was unable to pay her late husband's debts.

The king was unhappy with the education the new Prince of Wales was receiving, despite having hand-picked those responsible. A story reached him that the prince was being led astray into Jacobite sympathies. The accusation, made by Lord Harcourt, was directed at his recently appointed deputy, Andrew Stone. It was the princess's task to deny these accusations. She claimed that the way Harcourt had spoken to the boys had been disrespectful and insulting to their father, and that when they came to her, they had been 'almost ready to cry' (quoted by Waldegrave). George was in his early teens, his younger brother aged about ten. To cry at that age would have been no cause for shame. We need not doubt that cry in their mother's arms is exactly what they did. Whilst offering them maternal comfort, she refused to admit their weakness to an outsider.

Waldegrave, who had been appointed in place of the disgraced head of the Prince of Wales's household, was unimpressed with what he found, and put this down to the prince's having been brought up among women. In his memoirs, the earl claims that his motivation was 'to preserve harmony and union in the Royal Family', and indeed Augusta seemed to approve of him, though she admitted to Dodington that the whole idea of having a governor was 'a sort of pageant'. From this we glean the impression that she expected Waldegrave to have no lasting influence.

The princess, according to Dodington, confessed that her son needed to be 'a little more forward and less childish at his age', and that she considered both young princes to be 'backward', by which she appeared to mean that they were not at ease in society, rather than in any way intellectually lacking. On the other hand, she discouraged them from mixing, declaring to Dodington that 'young people of quality were so ill educated and so very vicious that they frightened her'. She was passing on her own basic insecurities to her eldest son.

Lady Louisa Stuart, a childhood companion of the prince, drew attention to the favouritism George's parents showed towards his brother, Edward; this was probably no more than the common tendency of parents to cosset a younger child whilst expecting great things of the eldest. In George's case, the tendency was exaggerated by the fact that he was destined to be king and needed training for the task. Once his father was no longer available to offer guidance, Augusta must have felt obliged to provide it herself. The only way she knew how to do this was to scold and dominate him. Lady Louisa claimed that, if the Prince of Wales ever ventured an opinion on anything, 'it was passed by unnoticed; sometimes knocked down at once with "Do hold your tongue, George: don't talk like a fool."'

Augusta was deeply suspicious of her brother-in-law, Cumberland, as well as of the king. Horace Walpole, in his memoirs, described how, when visiting Cumberland's home, George was shown a sword. 'The young prince turned pale and trembled, and thought his uncle was going to murder him. The duke was extremely upset and complained to the Princess of the impressions that had been instilled into the child against him.'

We see all the danger signs of an over-possessive, over-protective mother. The prince was being brought up almost in seclusion. Could this upbringing have influenced his development? Could it have had anything to do with the deteriorating mental condition that eventually led to his own son's having to assume the role of regent? George II soon tried to arrange a marriage between his grandson and a German princess, Sophia Caroline, elder daughter of the Duchess of Brunswick-Wolfenbüttel, whom he had met during his visit to Hanover. Contemporary accounts suggest that the king, who always had an eye for the ladies, was himself attracted to the girl, but, at seventy-two, had the sense to realize that it would not do.

The king's intention was to dilute the influence of the dowager Princess of Wales, but she successfully turned the prospective bridegroom against the idea. She wanted an alliance with her own home province of Saxe-Gotha, although later she would allow her daughter to marry into the Brunswick family. The king, on ministerial advice, offered the prince an allowance of

£40,000 a year to enable him to set up his own household at St James's. For political purposes, he would come of age in the summer of 1756, but would not be entitled to such freedom until he reached his twenty-first birthday. The prince took the money, but stayed with his mother. In the country as in London, the Prince of Wales had his own house: Richmond Lodge, in the grounds of what would become Kew Palace but was then known as the White House. This was where he was staying when the news arrived of his grandfather's death.

Despite her determination to thwart the old king's wishes, Augusta was ready to accept advice from the prince's tutor, John Stuart, Earl of Bute, a friend of her late husband. The Butes were a Scottish aristocratic family. Later, they became connected with the city of Cardiff, when one of John Stuart's descendants married into a Welsh family. This was unconnected with Augusta's position as Princess of Wales.

In 1754 Bute bought a house on Kew Green in London and built an extension to accommodate his botanical library. The house had a private gate into the grounds of Kew Palace where the earl would help Augusta create the nucleus of today's Royal Botanic Gardens. The following year, Bute was appointed 'finishing tutor' to the future George III. In 1756 he became groom of the stole in Prince George's household. The dowager Princess of Wales may well have been attracted to Bute, who by all accounts was a good-looking man, a more suitable role model than the prince's father might have been. Bute was credited with 'the most elegant legs in London', but he was happily married, and his religious scruples would have been an obstacle to an affair with Augusta.

The relationship, innocent as it may have been, became the subject of gossip, fostered by people such as Horace Walpole, who had few good words for the princess, describing her as 'a passionate, domineering woman'. By today's standards, this sounds less of an insult than he intended. Nevertheless, Bute was disliked by the public, even when Augusta interfered in politics to help him into office. As Pitt's political ally, he had looked forward to achieving a leading position in government in his own right as soon as his young protégé took the throne. The subject was openly discussed by the Prince of Wales and his tutor in the years leading up to his grandfather's death and his accession. Bute and Pitt fell out when Bute realized that he was not truly part of the inner circle surrounding the great politician.

In 1761 Bute established a newspaper titled *The Briton* (edited by Frederick, Prince of Wales's friend, Tobias Smollett) as a propaganda device. An unimpressive public speaker, the earl's political progress was hampered by his Scottish blood (he was the first Scotsman to be prime minister) as well as the scandal attaching to his supposed relationship with Augusta. In 1762 a rival newspaper appeared: the *North Briton*, edited by the notorious John Wilkes. Bute and his administration were ridiculed, Bute himself being labelled 'the King's incompetent friend'. The *North Briton* was a highly successful satirical publication, comparable with *Private Eye*, and offered no mercy to leading public figures, including the dowager Princess of Wales. In April 1763 the controversial Issue 45 denounced the king's speech in praise of the recent Peace of Paris; the speech was identified as Bute's own composition.

Bute was forced to resign as prime minister. He was now effectively removed from the orbit of the king, but not from that of the dowager Princess of Wales. According to a story quoted in the journal of Charles Greville, George III later told his son that the last time he set eyes on the Earl of Bute was at Kew, some time between 1764 and 1766, when he visited Augusta and found that she had brought Bute to her house in order to secure an audience, telling him that there was 'somebody here who wishes very much to speak with you'. The king, indignant at being placed in such an embarrassing situation, castigated his mother for allowing Bute into her house. The resulting meeting ended in a heated argument, as a result of which George broke off contact with his former tutor, though he wrote letters to him well after this date. We can imagine the personal difficulty in which Augusta found herself, torn between a man to whom she felt she owed so much and her loyalty to her son and monarch.

Shortly after his accession, George married a German princess, Charlotte of Mecklenburg-Strelitz. At a stroke, Augusta was no longer the most important woman in the country. She is alleged to have installed her own personal spy, Katherine Dashwood, in the new queen's household, in order to receive regular reports. One wonders how she might have expected to catch Charlotte out. Was it simple curiosity, since Augusta had never herself been queen? Following the treatment she had sometimes suffered at the hands of Queen Caroline, she had found herself the first lady of the land when her mother-in-law died prematurely. She had been catapulted into the public eye, and when her husband followed his mother to the grave, she had no one to turn to. She had brought up her son, to the best of her ability, and had no wish to lose her influence over him.

Jokes about mothers-in-law are commonly made by male comedians, but in fact it is women who most often suffer the jealousy of a mother-in-law. Today the mothers of sons are more aware of this failing in themselves; in the eighteenth century, when few women had careers to occupy them, there was little hope of a royal princess recognizing the extent to which she might be contributing to the unhappiness of another, even when she had been through it herself.

Augusta's attitude towards her own children seems to have carried over into the family life of her son. The young king was soon a father, and a devoted and loving one, but with draconian opinions on upbringing. All the children, especially the girls, were kept isolated from others of their age, and had to follow strict rules of etiquette that threatened to stifle their individual development. Queen Charlotte seems to have approved of this, just as Augusta had always gone along with Frederick's domestic rulings. Whatever the relations between the queen and her mother-in-law, they saw one another regularly over the next ten years. At least twice a week, the young couple called on the dowager Princess of Wales.

Five years after George's accession, he was taken seriously ill with a fever, and the possibility of a regency arose, since his son, later to be King George IV, was an infant. The king himself began the controversy by proposing that, in the event of his being incapacitated or dying, he should be able to nominate the regent. This was not usual, as a Regency Act normally named the regent specifically. Although Augusta was not popular, she looked the most likely candidate to assume the power of the monarchy, for which role she had been approved fifteen years earlier. The alternatives were the young Queen Charlotte or the king's brother, Prince Edward, now Duke of York. Luckily, the king recovered, and the necessity never arose. His nomination, when he finally made it, was the queen, but it was stipulated that the dowager princess would assume the role in the event of Charlotte's death. George evidently had no confidence in his brother to carry out a regent's duties.

A bill was introduced, and much debated, in an attempt to cater for any future recurrence of this crisis. Parliament did not approve of Augusta as a potential regent. Eventually the words, 'born in England' were introduced into the bill, specifically to exclude the princess. The queen, who, like her mother-in-law, had been born in Germany, apparently qualified through marriage as a British subject. Walpole claims that, when the perceived slight against Augusta was pointed out to George, he spoke nervously to the prime minister, Grenville, about 'the mark of disregard shown to the Princess of Wales, his mother, by the words which excluded her alone from the Regency . . .'

Doubt has been expressed as to whether Augusta was really interested in the job. When her son was under age, she might have been concerned to ensure that he was not taken advantage of by others. In the five years since his accession, however, they had grown apart. They no longer lived in one another's pockets.

Augusta died at Carlton House, London, of cancer, at the age of fifty-two. A mob followed her body to the grave with cheers and insults. She had remained unpopular with people like Horace Walpole, and this public image was encouraged by the contemporary equivalent of the mass media. Only a year before her death, a Radical MP, James Townsend, got up in the House to describe her as 'the real cause of all the calamities which had befallen this country for these last ten unfortunate years . . .' Was Augusta aware of the bad press? What was its effect on her peace of mind?

In 1770 she had travelled abroad to visit her two married daughters: Augusta, at her home in Brunswick, and Caroline Matilda in Denmark. On this trip she was accompanied by her son William, Duke of Gloucester. By 1771, however, her cancer of the throat was well-advanced, and she had become a cantankerous old woman. In November, George wrote to William, his closest confidant, about their mother, saying 'it is impossible you can figure to yourself how much she is reduced since you went abroad'. William had himself been taken seriously ill while travelling in Italy, and had not been expected to live. This was another subject for his mother to concern herself with, following close on the heels of the naming of her youngest son, Henry, in a notorious divorce case.

As her illness reached a critical point, the king was seeing his mother four times a week, and reported back to his brother on her weight loss, incoherent speech and other failings. As a concession to her last wishes, he arranged for his eldest sister to return from Brunswick to visit their mother. By this time, the cancer of the throat had such a hold on the dowager princess that she could not speak at all. Describing the final hours of his mother's life, George wrote tenderly, but with relief, 'We had the melancholy scene of knowing she could not last, but that it must not be taken notice of as she did not choose to think so.'

In 1772, the same year that Augusta of Saxe-Gotha died, the youngest of her daughters, Caroline Matilda, Queen of Denmark, was divorced for adultery, at the age of only twenty-one. George III succeeded in having her released from confinement (though she was deprived of her children), and she was allowed to travel to Hanover. It was ironic that Caroline's downfall should have come about through a situation similar to that which had caused her mother's unpopularity. Unable to form a relationship with her mad husband, the Danish queen had turned to an advisor, Struensee, the court physician. Struensee, like the Earl of Bute, had political ambitions, and brought Caroline down with him.

George's eldest sister, Augusta, remained married to Duke Charles II of Brunswick-Wolfenbüttel. They were the parents of Caroline of Brunswick, who was to be the next, and most infamous, Princess of Wales.

Caroline of Brunswick (1768–1821)

George Augustus Frederick, born in 1762 to George III and Charlotte of Mecklenburg-Strelitz, grew into an attractive and talented young man, as prodigal with his affections as in his expenditure. In 1784 he secretly married Mrs Maria Fitzherbert, a devout Roman Catholic widow who had refused to become his mistress. She does not become our next Princess of Wales; the marriage was illegal under the terms of the Royal Marriages Act, which had come into force only twelve years previously. It was just as well, for after a while the prince tired of Mrs Fitzherbert, and was tempted to take a legal Protestant wife in order to obtain an extra financial allowance from Parliament. At this point the prince decided to marry his first cousin (the daughter of his father's sister), whom he had never set eyes on. Caroline of Brunswick seemed an eminently suitable wife, but the tale of her married life is one of conflict and unhappiness.

She was born in May 1768, the daughter of the duke and duchess of the German province called Brunswick by the English, and her upbringing, though not abnormal by Hanoverian standards, did not equip her for her future role. Queen Charlotte was aware of Caroline's unsuitability, having already vetoed her as a match for her own brother. She commented on the fact that Caroline, at home in Brunswick, was strictly chaperoned. It was reported that, at dances, 'this Lady is obliged to follow her for the whole of the dance to prevent her making an exhibition of herself by indecent conversations with men'. The word 'conversations' is a euphemism. The information had reached the queen third-hand, and indelicate speech and behaviour was not unknown among the German nobility. Caroline, at the age of eighteen, was described by Honoré Mirabeau as 'most amiable, lively, playful, witty and handsome'.

Caroline of Brunswick, disgraced wife of the Prince Regent.
From a Victorian print.

A year after Mirabeau was introduced to the princess, Caroline's elder sister Augusta was deserted by her husband, making a good marriage for the younger sister a remote prospect. The king and Queen of Great Britain did not exactly favour the match with their son, but the prince was encouraged by his mistress, Lady Jersey, in his choice of wife. Jersey's aim was simply to remove, once and for all, the competition from Mrs Fitzherbert. According to the Duke of Wellington, she had picked Caroline out precisely because of her 'indelicate manners, indifferent character, and not very inviting appearance, from the hope that disgust for the wife would secure constancy to the mistress'.

Lord Malmesbury, who was sent to Brunswick to inspect and advise Caroline, recorded many impressions of her. Other observers reported that she did not wash properly or dress neatly, and had bad teeth. Malmesbury, partly out of kindness and partly out of concern for the royal family, offered her some guidance on her future conduct, recommending that she be 'affable, without forgetting she was Princess of Wales'. In other words, a future queen should not get too close to her subjects.

Despite having personally selected his bride, George was disappointed in her. He had, unwisely, sent Lady Jersey to greet Caroline on her arrival in England in 1795, and the result was that the princess's lack of looks was highlighted by some deliberately misleading advice on fashion and make-up. The prince immediately regretted his decision; his reported words on seeing her sum up the situation succinctly: 'I am not well, pray get me a glass of brandy' (quoted by Lord Malmesbury, the only witness to that first meeting). Nor was Caroline impressed with his appearance and manners. She observed, to Malmesbury, how fat the prince was, and nothing like as handsome as his portrait.

The marriage went ahead a few days later, though the prince was allegedly on the verge of calling it off. The couple were married on the evening of 8 April at the Chapel Royal in St James's Palace. Queen Charlotte arranged for the princess to be dressed for the wedding exactly as Augusta of Saxe-Gotha, her predecessor as Princess of Wales, had been for her wedding to Prince Frederick in 1736; that couple were the common grand-parents of this Prince and Princess of Wales. Caroline wore a gown of silver tissue and lace, and a velvet robe lined with ermine.

By now pining for Mrs Fitzherbert, George was too drunk to put himself to bed after the ceremony. He later told Malmesbury that the princess's manners 'were not those of a novice', implying that she was not a virgin. He also stated that her body was scarred and she did not wash her genital area, and claimed that they had sex a total of three times in those first few days, and not at all afterwards.

In her own diary, Caroline says that the prince tried to visit Mrs Fitzherbert a few days after the wedding. She later told the Earl of Minto that, after the first two or three weeks, she never lived with the prince as man and wife. She complained to Minto of his drinking and the company he kept. Lady Jersey controlled the household. In June, when the prince and princess removed to Brighton, the royal mistress came with them. Already Lady Sheffield was able to observe a marked change in Caroline: 'Her lively spirits, which she brought over with her, are all gone . . .'

George had wanted marriage because of the promise of an increase in his allowance, from £60,000 to £125,000, which would go towards paying off his enormous debts. When the proposal came before Parliament, Pitt was forced to increase the suggested amount from the prince's income and the revenues of the Duchy of Cornwall that would be set aside to pay the debt. The end result was that the prince would now have *less* disposable income than previously. This did not endear his new wife to him, and he took the opportunity to get rid of her attendants. The few intimate moments between them had done their work, however, for the princess was soon pregnant.

Caroline had to return to London, to Carlton House, for her confinement. The location carries echoes of previous royal unhappiness. It was here, in 1772, that the previous Princess of Wales had died, and here also that Princess Caroline Matilda 'of Wales' had married by proxy the King of Denmark, only to be divorced for adultery. At last Queen Charlotte took charge of Caroline's fate, though continuing to tolerate Lady Jersey as a companion in preference to her daughter-in-law. Princess Charlotte Augusta was born on the morning of 7 January 1796, and was given the Christian names of her two grandmothers. It was a difficult labour, and she was a large child.

Following the birth of his daughter, the overwrought prince imagined himself to be seriously ill. He made a new will, with this postscript: 'I forgot to mention that the jewels which she who is called the Princess of Wales wears are mine, having been bought with my own money . . . These I bequeath to my infant daughter as her own property, and to her who is called Princess of Wales I leave one shilling.' It seems that George's dislike of Caroline was now based on something more significant than physical disgust. Later he wrote that she 'is the vilest wretch this world was ever cursed with, who I cannot feel more disgust for from her personal nastiness than I do from her entire want of principle'.

Meanwhile, he wrote to his mother: 'Notwithstanding we might have wished for a boy, I receive her with all the affection possible, and bow . . . to the decrees of Providence.' This statement from the prince comes as a pleasant surprise, in marked contrast to the attitude of Henry VIII to his female children two centuries earlier. Times had changed. Not only was the Hanoverian dynasty more secure than the Tudors had ever been, but it was no longer deemed impossible for a lone woman to reign. From the beginning, the Prince of Wales tried to limit the child's contact with her mother. The 'Carlton House system' was his attempt to keep his wife under control. Princess Charlotte acquired two governesses. Frances Garth was about the same age as the Princess of Wales, and quickly became her friend. Together they took the baby on regular visits to the queen, who still had not warmed to Caroline. Ann Hayman, from Wrexham, replaced Miss Garth as governess, and became friendly with Caroline. The Prince of Wales, learning of their relationship, spitefully dismissed Miss Hayman, but she was reinstated as keeper of the 'privy purse' to the Princess of Wales.

It became common knowledge that Caroline wanted Lady Jersey removed from her household and that the royal couple were leading separate lives, apparently by mutual consent. Princess Charlotte was removed from her mother's influence, but this did not prevent the Princess of Wales from becoming an embarrassment to her husband by the time they had been married a year. Already the newspapers had picked up on it. *The Times* of 24 May referred obliquely to a 'separation in high life'. The king forbade an official separation – the princess was, after all, his niece as well as his daughter-in-law – and eventually Lady Jersey was forced to resign her official position, if not her unofficial one. There were signs of public sympathy for Caroline when she went to the opera in May 1796.

In the meantime, the prince's desire for a separation was thwarted. Malmesbury warned him that 'your parting from . . . the Princess of Wales would . . . involve your Royal Highness in difficulties, distresses, and I must add, dangers . . .' There are a number of things Malmesbury may have considered dangerous to the prince, including the potential loss of income and loss of face. George's own history was well known, but he shamelessly denied adultery, claiming that Lady Jersey was simply 'a friend'. He did, however, write politely to his estranged wife, pointing out that their mutual distaste could not be overcome by forcing themselves to live together. 'Our inclinations are not in our power . . . Tranquil and comfortable society is, however, in our power; let our intercourse therefore be restricted to that.'

The attempt at a reconciliation was purely a face-saving exercise, and the prince continued to exclude his wife from important public occasions, such as the thanksgiving service at St Paul's following the British victory at Camperdown towards the end of 1797. After this episode, she spoke to him for the first time in months, accusing him of treating her 'neither as your wife, nor the mother of your child, nor as the Princess of Wales'.

What did she mean by that last phrase? She could have known nothing of Wales, therefore she must have been alluding to the status which the title of Princess of Wales conferred upon her and the respect she was due as a future queen. Ironically, it was thanks to her subsequent conduct that the title, Princess of Wales, began to carry undertones of scandal, as it had done in the days of her grandmother, Augusta of Saxe-Gotha.

The following year, Caroline rejected her husband's feeble attempts at reconciliation, believing (no doubt correctly) that he had ulterior motives. The princess now had a separate household and began to entertain her own friends. One of those with whom she flirted was the up-and-coming politician, George Canning. Canning married in a hurry, avoiding potential scandal, but confessed that he had not been immune to her charms. 'I know not how I should have resisted, as I ought to do, the abundant and overpowering temptation . . . which must have been dangerous, perhaps ruinous, to her who was the cause of it . . .' Apparently he did not find her as repulsive as her husband did. Had she learned, as a result of the prince's rejection of her, to change her personal habits?

Caroline, now in her thirties, was living at Montague House in Blackheath, enjoying some social freedom. She could pay only occasional visits to her daughter, but by all accounts was devoted to Charlotte. The enforced separation led the princess to seek other outlets for her maternal instinct. She started a nursery in the district, for deprived local children. In 1802 a three-month-old baby boy, Willy Austin, turned up, and Caroline announced her intention of adopting him. His presence in her household would be the cause of scandal.

In 1801 George III, who had temporarily recovered from the mental condition that plagued him, started visiting Caroline, making the queen jealous and arousing the prince's resentment. He appointed her ranger of Greenwich Park, enabling her to dispose of property and enjoy a private income. After 1800, the Prince of Wales, claiming to be a reformed character, had resumed his relationship with Mrs Fitzherbert, and moved into a house near the Royal Pavilion with her; but when he acquired another mistress Mrs Fitzherbert would not agree to share him, so they parted again. The Princess of Wales continued to do her own thing.

We may regard Caroline of Brunswick as having been unlucky in being chosen as the wife of a man who, despite great natural abilities, never fulfilled his early promise, veered between great popularity and great unpopularity with his subjects, and became a byword for extravagance and loose living. She was not the first royal personage, or even the first Princess of Wales, to attract the attention of the press, but clear parallels may be drawn between her and some female members of the royal family in the twentieth century.

By 1802, she had taken a lover – an admiral, Sir Sidney Smith. An involvement with the portrait painter Thomas Lawrence was also the subject of rumour. Smith went out of favour when a humble sea captain, Thomas Manby, arrived on the scene.

According to Lord Glenbervie, this new admirer was not 'a person one could expect to meet in the society of a Princess of Wales'. Throughout this story, we note how the title, Princess of Wales, is used without any reference to Wales or interest in the principality as an entity. 'Wales', as used by the princess's contemporaries, is merely a word that makes up part of her official form of address, just as the term Knight of the Garter does not automatically make one think of a garter.

In 1804 Charles Abbot wrote: 'The Princess of Wales causes great uneasiness by her unguarded conduct.' In that same year, the princess sent anonymous, obscene letters to Sir John and Lady Douglas, apparently because she was jealous of their involvement with her ex-lover, Smith. Looking back on these episodes in the light of history, one wonders whether Caroline believed herself immune from discovery or punishment, simply because of her status. It is equally possible that she had been so buffeted by the vagaries of fortune that she no longer felt she had anything to lose.

Princess Charlotte's conduct was giving cause for concern. Her education was not going well; she misbehaved and told lies. She lived with her royal grandparents at Windsor, where her mother continued to visit her. Determined to dispense with Caroline, her husband had accumulated circumstantial evidence against her. In June 1806 George III, despite personal affection for his daughter-in-law, allowed a secret investigation by a committee of Cabinet ministers into her conduct and the possible existence of an illegitimate child, an accusation made by Lady Douglas in retaliation for Caroline's anonymous letters. Other insinuations were made, even one of a lesbian relationship. The princess was accused of having committed adultery with Captain Manby, which was probably true.

Several servants and former servants of the Blackheath household gave evidence, some siding with the prosecution and some with the defence. Fortunately for Caroline, the committee was not disposed to find against her, and the results of the investigation were not made public. They reported to the king that the princess had not given birth to Willy Austin or any other illegitimate baby, but that she had kept lovers. The king responded by cutting off close relations. The Prince of Wales now accepted that, since the only way he could get a divorce was by proving adultery in court, he had better let sleeping dogs lie. His wife had threatened to retaliate by producing evidence of his adultery, something he dared not risk.

Besides her isolated state, the Princess of Wales had many reasons to be unhappy. She was involved in a serious carriage accident in 1806. Her elder brother Charles died, followed by her father, who had been wounded while resisting Napoleon's invasion of Brunswick. In 1808, she moved into Kensington Palace, using the former apartments of one of her predecessors, Caroline of Ansbach. There she formed her own social circle, until forced to move out three years later by her husband, who now ruled the country as regent.

As Prince of Wales, George IV was one of the few since medieval times to pay an official visit to the land from which he took his title. By the time he did so, in 1806, he was already separated from his princess, and we cannot credit her with having taken any personal interest. The prince, on the other hand, seems to have developed a fondness for his principality. Later, as king, he toyed with the idea of creating a special order of knighthood, that of St David, especially for Wales. This idea would be shelved by his successor on the throne, his brother William, who had never been Prince of Wales and had no such sentiments.

In 1811 the prince gave a party to celebrate his regency, failing to invite either his first, illegal wife, Maria Fitzherbert, or his legal wife, the Princess of Wales. The prince's sisters refused to recognize the new royal mistress, Lady Conyngham, on the stated grounds that they had been forbidden to speak to his wife, the Princess of Wales, and therefore could not possibly acknowledge his mistress. This was a feeble excuse; they had never hesitated to socialize with his previous mistresses. The truth was that they disliked Lady Conyngham even more than they disliked Caroline.

George took advantage of his new powers by forbidding his wife from seeing their daughter more than once a fortnight. Princess Charlotte, their only heir, fell out with both parents in her teens, for the usual reasons, but this would not bring the couple any closer. Caroline, aware of her husband's unpopularity, took a step which an earlier Princess of Wales, Katherine of

Aragon, had taken in similar circumstances, and made a public appeal for sympathy. In 1813 she wrote a letter that was printed in a Whig newspaper, the *Morning Chronicle*, almost the equivalent of a *Panorama* interview today. The letter contained no confessions of wrongdoing. It addressed the Prince of Wales directly, reminding him of the respect due to her as 'the mother of your daughter – the mother of her who is destined, I trust at a very distant period, to reign over the British Empire'. So strongly did she appeal to female fellow-feeling that the novelist Jane Austen, reading her words, remarked: 'I shall support her as long as I can, because she is a woman, and because I hate her husband.'

Caroline had moved to Connaught Place. She had grown fat and lost what looks she ever possessed. In June 1814 she appeared at Covent Garden, attending an opera at which her husband was also present. The prince deftly stole the applause intended for his wife; but afterwards she was surrounded by well-wishers. Nothing could heal the rift between them, and there was no one to whom the Princess of Wales could turn, as long as George remained regent.

After the breaking of Princess Charlotte's engagement to William of Orange, it was to her mother that the teenage girl came for comfort, only to be hurt when she learned that Caroline was making plans to leave England. She did so later in 1814. Caroline would be travelling in Italy, where she spent most of the years between then and her estranged husband's succession to the throne, when she learned of her daughter's engagement to Leopold of Saxe-Coburg. She was not invited to the wedding at Carlton House. Their forcible separation over the years had succeeded in breaking down any last vestiges of a natural mother–daughter relationship.

By now, Caroline was accumulating huge debts and was unwelcome almost everywhere in Europe, rapidly becoming a figure of fun. She was never officially informed of Princess Charlotte's death in 1817, from complications following the stillbirth of her first child. The news reached Caroline second-hand, from a passing messenger. There was no hope of ever regaining respectability; there would not even be a grandchild. Caroline's only supporter was her lover, Bartolomeo Pergami, the chamberlain of her household. He may have entered the relationship expecting to profit from Caroline's connections with the British royal family; if so, he must have been disappointed. Her behaviour had gone to such extremes that her husband successfully built up a dossier which he planned to use to obtain the long-awaited divorce. Left without an heir, he attempted to start proceedings so that he could remarry.

The prince, although he was regent, received no support from the government for divorce action. In 1820 Caroline, hearing that her father-in-law was dead and she was now, technically, queen of Great Britain, made a precipitate decision to return to her realm. A 'queenite' faction emerged to welcome her, born out of widespread disapproval of her husband rather than any affection for her. The new king's determination not to recognize his wife was such that a parliamentary bill was read in an attempt to remove her titles. The subsequent revelations lost her much public sympathy. Proceedings continued in the House of Lords, but the bill ultimately failed.

A popular rhyme summed up the public attitude:

> Most Gracious Queen, we thee implore,
> To go away and sin no more,
> Or if that effort is too great,
> To go away at any rate.

The new 'queen' might not have been an object of hatred, but she remained an object of derision, unable to resist her husband's continued denial of her. On coronation day, in the summer of 1821, she was turned away from the doors of Westminster Abbey. Publicly humiliated and reviled, Caroline's health had been completely destroyed by her ordeal. She died within a few weeks, possibly as a result of dosing herself with unsuitable medicines. The new king was in Anglesey, making the first state visit to Wales and Ireland by a British monarch. His reaction to the news of Caroline's death was one of shock as well as relief, and he never remarried. The body of the former Princess of Wales was returned to Brunswick for burial.

Interest in Caroline's life was suddenly renewed at the time of the separation and divorce of the present Prince of Wales and his wife. Biographers and television script-writers began to depict her as a near-twin and role model of Diana, Princess of Wales. The reality is that they were two very different women, whose lives happened to follow certain common paths, relating directly to their position as Princess of Wales, wife of the heir to the throne. Neither was able to defend herself effectively against the pressures of living in the public eye whilst enduring an unhappy marriage. Caroline of Brunswick lived in an era when marriage for love was not a real option for a woman of her station, yet she resisted the pressure to conform. Whether this was from unusual strength of character or unusual stupidity is difficult to decide.

Ironically, the next Princess of Wales, though born in a different century, would also face the ordeal of marriage to a man who was incapable of fidelity.

Alexandra of Denmark (1844–1925)

When the Sandringham estate workers marched out to join the First World War effort, they had the personal support and interest of the queen mother. She had a particular reason to hate the Germans, because she was Danish by birth. She had been queen for nine years, and she was queen mother for a further fifteen. But it was as Princess of Wales that she had become associated with Sandringham, and she had held that title for nearly forty years. Alexandra of Denmark was the wife of 'Bertie', that seemingly everlasting Prince of Wales.

Alix, as she was known, was born in December 1844, in Copenhagen. Her parents were Prince Christian, heir to the throne of Denmark (an outside candidate for the hand of the young Queen Victoria), and his wife, Princess Louise. Christian became known as 'the father-in-law of Europe', because of the prestigious marriages made by his many children. Alix and her younger sister, Dagmar or 'Minnie', were brought up by loving, but not wealthy, parents. Christian was in line for the throne only because of the childlessness of the existing Danish king, and the family lived on his army pay, in the unpretentious Amalienborg or Yellow Palace. As a child, Alix's stated ambition was 'to be loved', no great challenge for one of her looks and temperament.

Bertie had caused his family great concern. His flirtations were an indirect cause of the death of his father, Prince Albert, who virtually worried himself into the grave over his eldest son's behaviour. Alix and Bertie were introduced by his sister, Princess Victoria, wife of the Prussian ruler, while he was touring Europe in September 1861. She had been recommended by Vicky's friend, Countess von Hothenthal, who described her as

Alexandra, Princess of Wales, shortly after her marriage to the future King Edward VII. From a Victorian print.

'a half-open rosebud'. Bertie had previously seen a photograph of Alix. Captivated by her in the full colour of life, he soon had her marked out as his princess. There were no communication difficulties, as the princess spoke English fluently. Contemporary photographs show how attractive Alix was. Even as a teenager, she was considered to have regal bearing. Although her family had a more energetic and less stuffy lifestyle than the British royals, her health was imperfect. Later, she suffered premature deafness, which she called her 'beastly ears'; this weakness would pass to her eldest son.

Much has been said about the impression Alix made on Bertie, but little about how Bertie may have appeared to Alix at their early meetings. The prince was stout and hardly handsome. For Alix's parents, a match between their daughter and the future king of Great Britain was a dream come true. For Alix herself, the process of courtship under the eyes of both royal families must have been an ordeal. Yet she seems to have had no hesitation in accepting the proposal when it was made, in the royal gardens at Brussels.

The prince's mother, Queen Victoria, was unsure about a match with a Danish princess, preferring the idea of a German daughter-in-law. Baron von Stockmar, Prince Albert's former mentor, had warned that he believed Bertie was being rushed into marriage for the wrong reasons. 'The main reason for this affair,' wrote the baron,

> was given to me that it is hoped that the defects of spirit and mind of the one person should be made up by the strength of the other person. How daring would it be to take part in this lottery of possibilities . . . Not a step further, otherwise a disaster can occur of which the consequences cannot be foreseen.

Stockmar's fears, if not groundless, were never realized. Victoria was won over after meeting Alexandra in person; the princess had a 'quiet ladylike manner'. It was shortly afterwards that Bertie proposed and was accepted. At the same time, Victoria, in a private interview with Alix's parents, discussed the practical side. Her diary reveals her conflicting emotions as they discussed the engagement:

> I said that I trusted their dear daughter would feel, should she accept our son, that she was doing so with her whole heart and will. They assured me that Bertie might hope she would do so, and that they trusted he also felt a real inclination, adding that they hoped God would give their dear child strength to do what she ought, and that she

might be able to pour some comfort into my poor heart, that they were sure she would become quickly attached to me, and be a good wife to Bertie.

The queen enlisted the aid of her ex-prime minister, Earl Russell, to ensure the political acceptability of the marriage, overcoming the opposition of Britain's German connections. The Germans were at odds with the Danes over the provinces of Schleswig and Holstein, and reluctant to see the British royal family allied with Denmark. The decisive factor was that Victoria came to believe that her late husband would have approved of the match. Albert (who, like his son, had been impressed by Alexandra's portrait) had died of typhoid shortly after a family quarrel resulting from Bertie's affair with an actress. Today we remember Victoria as an old woman, but she was only in her early forties when she was widowed. She was still in mourning at the time of the prince's marriage in March 1863, though Albert had been dead for well over a year. Her unwillingness to be consoled cast a small shadow over the wedding celebrations.

The Times announced the royal engagement on 16 September 1862, in words that bore the stamp of the queen's authorship:

We understand that the marriage of the Prince of Wales to the Princess Alexandra of Denmark . . . is based entirely on mutual affection and the personal merit of the young Princess, and is in no way connected with political consideration. The late Prince Consort, whose sole object was the welfare and happiness of his children, had long been convinced that this was a most suitable marriage. The knowledge of this is in itself a sense of deep gratification to the Queen, and will be as such satisfactory to the country.

Alix's veneer of sedateness and good breeding had won over the queen, but underneath she was light-hearted and fun-loving, and this tendency never left her in adulthood. To entertain Bertie's younger siblings, she turned a cartwheel at Windsor Castle, presumably when the queen was not looking. Another story tells how she charmed Tennyson, who in his capacity as Poet Laureate had composed an extremely formal ode in her honour:

> Sea Kings' daughter from over the sea,
>   Alexandra,
> Saxon and Norman and Dane are we
> But all of us Danes in our welcome of thee,
>   Alexandra!

The 'Celt' is mentioned only once, in the penultimate line of this long rambling poem of greeting.

The future Princess of Wales arrived in Britain in the autumn of 1862, in order to familiarize herself with the country and with court protocol. Although she preferred non-intellectual pursuits, Alix took care to do what was necessary to retain Victoria's approval, taking lessons in English and drawing. She won the queen's favour by showing genuine emotion when listening to her reminiscences about Prince Albert. Victoria was delighted with Alix's progress, but made no special concessions. It was decreed that she should have no Danish ladies-in-waiting, and the prince was not to visit Denmark before the wedding. Throughout their time as an engaged couple, the prince and princess were chaperoned, and Alix returned home for the last few months of her engagement.

The queen's true feelings about Alix were revealed in a letter to her daughter, Princess Vicky, shortly before the wedding: 'She is one of those sweet creatures who seem to come from the skies to help and bless poor mortals and brighten for a time their path.' Alix's second trip to Britain in March 1863 was quite different from the first, awkward, encounter. This time she arrived on the royal yacht, the *Victoria and Albert*, to be welcomed by cheering crowds at Gravesend. Flowers were strewn in the road as the young couple walked to their train. The marriage took place three days later, at St George's Chapel (where they would one day be buried). True to form, Queen Victoria had overseen every detail, including music composed by her late husband, and the design of the wedding dress, of silver tissue trimmed with Honiton lace. The queen viewed the ceremony from 'Katherine of Aragon's closet'.

Several guests described Alexandra's appearance as that of a fairytale princess, a phrase that echoes down to another royal wedding: that of 1981. The novelist, Charles Dickens, who was a wedding guest, wrote: 'The Princess's face was very pale and full of a sort of awe and wonder. It was the face of no ordinary bride, not simply a timid, shrinking girl, but one with a distinctive character of her own, prepared to act a part greatly.' The Prince of Wales had lavished jewels worth £15,000 on his bride, and her wedding ring was set with stones whose initials spelled his name – Beryl, Emerald, Ruby, Turquoise, Jacinth and Emerald. William Powell Frith was commissioned to paint a famous picture of the occasion, for a fee of £3,000. Photography, though technologically possible, was out of the question.

The couple's obvious happiness did not prevent criticism of the wedding arrangements, particularly the location. *Punch* commented:

> As it is now finally settled that the marriage of the Prince of Wales is not to take place in London, but in an obscure village in Berkshire, remarkable only for an old castle and non-sanitary arrangements, Mr Punch ventures to suggest that the secrecy of the proceeding should be carried out to the utmost...

Others, taking the opposite view, were concerned with the cost of the occasion. A left-wing organ, *Reynolds's Newspaper*, described Alexandra as 'an inanimate doll, for fashion to ape and extravagance to deck'. Evidently, some people were already sick of royal weddings.

Following the ceremony, Alix changed into white velvet for the couple's departure on honeymoon. They were seen off at the railway station by schoolboys from nearby Eton. One of these, Lord Randolph Churchill, described to his parents how he broke through the police cordon: 'I got right down to the door of the carriage where the Prince of Wales was, wildly shouting "Hurrah!" I am sure, if the Princess did not possess very strong nerves, she would have been frightened. But all she did was to smile . . .' In later years, Bertie, Alix and Lord Randolph would come to know one another only too well.

The event, together with Bertie's coming of age and investiture as Prince of Wales not long before, was the subject of great public celebration. At the Caernarfon Eisteddfod of 1862 the idea of a special anthem was put forward, and it was written by the time of the wedding, with music by Henry Brinley Richards, and Welsh words by the poet Ceiriog (John Hughes). 'Ar Dywysog Gwlad y Bryniau', translated into English as 'God Bless the Prince of Wales', achieved great popularity. It is still sung on appropriate occasions. Another musician called upon to honour the new princess was Sir Arthur Sullivan, whose contribution was 'Princess of Wales March on Danish Airs' or 'Marche Danoise'. Performed by military bands to greet Alexandra's arrival in London for her wedding, it was one of two marches Sullivan wrote for the occasion, in addition to a song called 'Bride From the North'.

Alexandra was eighteen at the time of her marriage, and Bertie only twenty-one. His conduct had made his parents anxious to see him safely married off to a suitable bride as soon as possible (though in the event, this would not put a permanent end to his philandering). The vivacious Alexandra quickly gained popularity, partly at the expense of her mother-in-law, who was little seen in public. Thus the princess was emulating Caroline of Ansbach, who, a hundred and fifty years earlier, had been welcomed by the British public as a substitute for the queen they felt they *should* have had.

The couple's first home was Marlborough House, soon the centre of a fashionable set. Their second home was Sandringham in Norfolk, a house bought by Prince Albert shortly before his death to be used for shooting-parties. Though sadly in need of attention, it made the ideal country residence for the royal newly-weds. Bertie and Alix gave it a complete makeover, and it became their refuge from public life and their favourite place for entertaining. The 'Sandringham Season' became a noted winter social event. Mrs Gladstone, who had begun life as Catherine Glynne of Hawarden in Flintshire, would report back to her husband, the prime minister, on Sandringham's delightful simplicity. Mr Gladstone had devised a 'plan of life' for the Prince of Wales, intended to help him prepare for kingship, but Victoria refused to allow him to interfere. She was so besotted with Benjamin Disraeli that anything suggested by his rival was ignored.

The queen still worried about her son's lifestyle after his marriage, and her disapproval extended to her new daughter-in-law. Even after the birth of her first child, Alix continued to enjoy society.

She was, after all, not yet in her twenties. Her most serious short-comings seem to have been her lack of punctuality and financial irresponsibility. The queen gradually became less complimentary in speaking of her to others, criticizing her looks, her behaviour, and her lack of savoir faire. Victoria expected to rule her son after his marriage, exactly as she had done before.

The princess was scarcely ready for so much public attention. Her own parents, though royalty, were in financial difficulties, and the prestige of the Danish royal family could hardly be compared with that of the Prince and Princess of Wales. (The King of Denmark had not even been invited to the wedding.) That did not discourage British ladies from scrambling to be presented to her at the palace. An American observer wrote:

> Nearly three thousand ladies paid their respects or were presented and it was long after five o'clock before the ceremony was over . . . The poor girl was absolutely exhausted; I may say that it was barbarous to impose so much upon her and none but the English people would have done it.

Bertie's younger brother Prince Alfred was one of his new sister-in-law's greatest admirers, following her around so doggedly that the queen had to stop him visiting Marlborough House.

In the past, Alix had been skilled at dressmaking, and her mother would walk about the streets of Copenhagen without an escort. Beauty and natural elegance enabled the new Princess of Wales to overcome what British royal circles perceived as the handicap of her family background and to be accepted as a leader of fashion and an example to female society in Britain. The living allowance of £40,000 a year granted the prince by Parliament was far beyond any budget Alix had ever expected to manage. The sum allocated to her as pin money alone was five times her father's income. In recognition of this, she arranged to share her dowry of 100,000 kroner with other Danish brides. Despite having been brought up to make do and mend, she quickly learned how to spend money, largely for the benefit of others. Before long, she was ordering her clothes from Worth's Paris studio. She owned three pianos, two carriages for everyday use, and could give orders to eighty-five servants at Marlborough House alone.

While Bertie and Alix were still getting used to their new status, Alix's teenage brother, Prince William George of Denmark, was elected King of Greece. No sooner were the negotiations complete than the King of Denmark died and Alix's father succeeded to the throne.

Six children were born to the Prince and Princess of Wales in the course of their long marriage. The first, Albert Victor Christian Edward (later created Duke of Clarence and always known as 'Eddy'), arrived less than a year after the marriage. Before Eddy's birth, Alix had been out on Virginia Water watching her husband play ice hockey, and she had to be rushed home by sledge and attended to by a local GP.

Public expectations were high. Even before the premature arrival, *Punch* had published a cartoon entitled 'What the Nation hopes soon to see', which depicted Queen Victoria holding her grandson in her arms. The queen had been anxious, before the birth, about the likely intellectual capacity of her grandchildren, bearing in mind her daughter-in-law's small head and her son's 'small empty brain'. She wrote to her eldest daughter, Vicky: 'The doctor says that Alix's head goes in, in the most extra-ordinary way just behind the forehead.' We may laugh, but this seems to have been a serious fear on Victoria's part. When the baby was born, in the worst mother-in-law tradition, she dictated all arrangements for the christening, down to the choice of names. (She had already commanded Bertie to ascend the throne as 'King Albert Edward', so as to commem-orate, but not compete with, his late father.)

By the time their second and third children were born, the Prince of Wales had learned to stand up to his mother. Learning from experience, Alix developed a habit of misleading the queen about her expected confinement date, to prevent Victoria from turning up to direct operations. The second son, George, who, by a quirk of fate, was to succeed his father as king, followed soon after the first. These two boys turned out to have very contrasting characters, but one thing they shared was an inordinate love for their mother. Then came three daughters, the youngest of whom, Maud, became Queen of Norway, and finally a son who died shortly after his birth. Alexandra, as was expected of a nineteenth-century princess, employed a wet-nurse, but looked after the children herself. She was a loving mother, who, unlike some of her predecessors, lavished time and attention on her family. Nowhere is this more clearly shown than in the grief she showed on the death of her eldest son in 1892, despite the fact that Eddy had caused his parents more worry than the rest of their children put together.

Alix's frequent pregnancies in the first few years of marriage made it difficult for her to get about with Bertie. Despite his frequent absences, she managed to maintain a warm family atmosphere. She composed birthday verses for the children to recite to their father, and she took them everywhere with her. They called her 'Motherdear', and she amused them with such antics as her habit of sliding downstairs using a tea-tray as a toboggan. She cared personally for the family's pet dogs, and in her private apartments at Sandringham she kept a white parrot, named 'Cocky', which she had taught to say 'God save the Queen'. The children's behaviour, by Victorian standards, was outrageous – in other words, normal.

As tutor to their sons, the prince and princess employed a Welshman, Canon Dalton (whose son, Hugh, would one day be chancellor of the exchequer). At Sandringham, under Dalton, the boys rose at seven, had lessons before breakfast, lessons after breakfast, lunch at two, and sport in the afternoon. Then there were more lessons until bed at eight o'clock. Despite, or perhaps because of, this rigorous régime, Dalton was soon expressing concern over Eddy's progress. He was convinced that the boy had some physical handicap, perhaps a degree of deafness inherited from his mother.

Alix was distressed by European politics. The Prussians were disputing the territory of Schleswig-Holstein, and Queen Victoria approved her government's refusal to assist the Danes. Bertie loyally took the Danish side, but had little influence on his mother, who refused to recognize that, as future king, he needed to be introduced to political as well as other official duties. Victoria disapproved of the young couple's visit to Denmark and Sweden in 1864, and tried to prevent it. Her private comments reveal that she regretted having allowed a marriage alliance with the Scandinavians, although she did not show it openly to her daughter-in-law: 'Alix, good as she is, is not worth the price we have had to pay for her in having such a family connection. I shall not readily let them go there again.'

Illness and depression followed the birth of Alix's first daughter, Louise, in 1867. An anxious crowd gathered outside Marlborough House, believing that the Princess of Wales was dying. She was suffering from 'white leg', a thrombosis which left her permanently lame, and there were no drugs to alleviate her condition. Her husband's neglect did not help. After her recovery, she remained slim and beautiful, but had to walk with a stick. Most noticeable was the deterioration in her hearing. There is no suggestion that Bertie was not a good father and loving husband, but he was still young, and avoided the sickroom. His mother-in-law, now Queen of Denmark, after visiting Britain, commented that Alix was making herself ill by conform-ing to Bertie's lifestyle. The prince, undaunted by his declining popularity, had set up his own club, directly opposite Marlborough House, where he could make his own rules and misbehave without fear of expulsion. Meanwhile, Alix recovered from her bout of rheumatic fever at the cost of a chronic stiffness of the joints.

Five years after their marriage, Bertie and Alix finally got around to visiting Wales, and were given a rousing welcome at Caernarfon Castle. They were en route to Ireland, where the prince was being sent by his mother to put a stop to his gadding about. Royal visits to the principality, even by the couple who 'ruled' it, were almost as rare as they had been in the Middle Ages. Yet Bertie's tenure as Prince of Wales was so long that he became known at home and abroad chiefly by that title. His activities, especially his friendships with numerous glamorous women, did not make him an ideal ambassador, and the princess did not always do better; her private secretary, Holzmann, was partly responsible for the anti-Prussian feeling that often surfaced. So great was her hatred for things German that the princess would have to be coerced by Queen Victoria into attending the funeral of the Kaiser in 1888.

Bertie's conduct towards married women sometimes got him into more public difficulties. In 1870 he was called to give evidence in a divorce case. Sir Charles Mordaunt's wife Harriet claimed to have had an affair with the prince, among others. For once, Bertie was innocent, and could prove it; nevertheless he had to stand in the witness box in full public view and give his testimony. This upset, coupled with mounting republican feeling in the country which caused the Prince and Princess of Wales to be booed in public, contributed to Alix's poor health. An indirect result was that her youngest child, Prince Alexander, was born premature and lived only twenty-four hours. After less than ten years of marriage, the Prince and Princess of Wales gave up sleeping together.

Alix, never short of admirers, found a particular friend in Oliver Montagu, a son of the Earl of Sandwich. Montagu was a surrogate uncle to her children, a reliable dancing partner, and even accompanied the prince and princess on holidays abroad. But the middle of the nineteenth century was quite different from its beginning; unlike the previous Princess of Wales and her lovers, neither Alix nor Montagu would have dared attempt to take the friendship further. Being worshipped from afar could not make up for the shortcomings in the princess's marriage.

The next blow was that Bertie himself was taken ill with typhoid, a killer disease rife in Britain in the nineteenth century (and which had killed his father). The prince's delirium was such that he failed to recognize his wife, but this did not prevent her maintaining a bedside vigil. She insisted on doing much of the caring herself, an action typical of a woman who would be remembered in years to come for her tireless charity work. Soon, Queen Victoria arrived at Sandringham to see for herself how Bertie was. Bertie's sister, Princess Alice, fancied herself as a nurse and belittled her sister-in-law's efforts, but her unkind words were no deterrent. When a servant was taken ill with typhoid, Alix looked after him as well as her husband.

Princess Alice having pronounced that death was imminent, Bertie rallied. Early in 1872, a thanksgiving service for his recovery helped restore the popularity of the royal family. A public holiday was declared, to allow people to attend celebrations throughout Britain. Bands everywhere played 'God Bless the Prince of Wales', and commemorative photographs of the prince and princess were a popular souvenir. Afterwards, Alix confided in her sister-in-law that Bertie's recovery had brought a new bloom to their marriage: 'You would hardly know me now in my happiness. We are never apart and are enjoying our second honeymoon.' To a friend, she wrote: 'This quiet time we two have spent here together now has been the happiest days of my life . . . we are both so happy to be left alone by ourselves.'

Even the queen noticed the change: 'There is something different which I can't exactly express . . . He is constantly with Alix and they seem hardly ever apart.' The couple toured the Continent, and on their return held a huge fancy-dress party to celebrate with friends. Bertie became a more enthusiastic father, even leaving the House of Lords early with the excuse that he had to take his wife and children to the circus. There was much comment on the unruly behaviour of the 'wild Wales children', who were given far more freedom than Bertie and his siblings had enjoyed. At Sandringham, the princess allowed them to associate with the children of the village, where she was known to the local women as 'Our Missus'. It was Alix who began the tradition of attendance at the village church, where the congregation admired her appearance and her readiness to offer favours.

The children's education, however, was sadly lacking. Their father had never been the most successful student, even under the eagle eye of Prince Albert, and Alix was even less academic-ally inclined. Queen Victoria deemed it of great importance that the two eldest boys should be properly educated, and it was she who had engaged Canon Dalton as tutor. Eddy's progress was still giving cause for concern. He could not work at all unless his brother George was there to urge him on. Both boys were sent to Dartmouth Naval College, where both were bullied. The navy would be the making of George, but it did little for Eddy. Their mother missed them desperately; throughout their lives she was reluctant to be parted from them, even for the shortest time.

Next Bertie took a notion to visit India on the queen's behalf, but Alix was prevented from accompanying him. This was one of the few occasions during their marriage when they were separated for any length of time. Public relations experts like Sir William Knollys always expressed concern when the couple were apart, fearing public comment. In the course of his trip, Bertie visited the Taj Mahal (shades of another Prince and Princess of Wales) and witnessed the naming of a new bridge in honour of his wife. While he was away, Lord Randolph

Churchill revealed to the princess the existence of letters from her husband to Lady Aylesford, whose husband happened to be in India at the time. Aylesford was threatening to sue for divorce because of his wife's affair with Churchill's brother, but the lady had been busier than anyone imagined. The Prince of Wales hurried home, and the correspondence, when available for inspection, turned out to be relatively innocent, but it was the start of a long-running feud with Churchill.

In 1888 the Prince and Princess of Wales celebrated their silver wedding anniversary with a dinner party at Marlborough House, where everyone commented on the princess's youthful appearance. A few years earlier, she had been introduced to the Zulu king, Cetewayo, who had been captured and brought to London to see the queen. At Marlborough House, he had asked for the Princess of Wales, and, according to Edward Hamilton, 'declined to believe that the lovely young woman he saw before him was the mother of such tall children'.

Their daughters were now reaching marriageable age, and the eldest, Princess Louise, made a surprising choice of husband – the Marquess of Macduff, nearly twenty years her senior. Her grandmother approved, and so, more surprisingly, did Alexandra. Louise became Duchess of Fife, and the first grandchild arrived soon afterwards. Most women in early middle age who took such pains with their own appearance would not have relished becoming a grandmother, but the Princess of Wales was thrilled, and remarked: 'At five o'clock . . . I held my little naked grandchild in my arms! It squeaked like a little sucking-pig.' The baby, a girl, was named Alexandra, in honour of both her father and her grandmother. Queen Victoria wrote: '. . . it is a very nice plump baby I hear. Alix is quite delighted to be a Grandmama.'

Alix's second daughter, Victoria, always known as 'Toria' at home, was not short of suitors, but none met with her mother's approval. She never did marry, and this has sometimes been put down to Alix's unwillingness to let her favourite daughter go. Alix's Danish family had gained in prestige over the years since her marriage. The Princess of Wales remained close to them all, despite geographical separation, and took every opportunity to see them. In 1891 she visited Russia, where her brother-in-law, Minnie's husband, had succeeded to the throne after the assassination of his predecessor. When Queen Victoria protested at the length of her stay in Russia, Alix's response was infuriatingly casual: 'It really was very kind of my Bertie to let me stop . . . it would have mattered much less if anything had happened to me than to him! Besides, I think one is bound to try and help those who are near and dear to us.'

In the travelling done by the Prince and Princess of Wales, the principality did not figure. It was the queen who visited Llangollen in 1889, and she gave Sir Henry Ponsonby a message for Bertie:

> . . . to tell him how much this naturally sensitive and warmhearted people feel the neglect shown them by the Prince of Wales and his family, and that it really is very wrong of him not to come here. It is only five hours from London, and as the Prince of Wales takes his title from this country, which is so beautiful, it does seem very wrong that neither he nor his children have come here often, and indeed, the Princess and the children not at all . . .

Extraordinary words from a sovereign whose name has become a byword for a stuffy and remote style of monarchy! Although the habit of ignoring Wales had not died out, there was at last some recognition by the royal family that the title of Prince of Wales ought to carry with it some sense of responsibility. It should also be noted that this was Victoria's first visit to Wales since becoming queen.

Alix and Bertie were in their element when entertaining at Sandringham. The Princess of Wales selected her guests carefully, favouring big names in the arts, such as Sir Arthur Sullivan and Charles Kingsley. She cared little for social origins and was unimpressed by titles, telling Mrs Gladstone: 'When I think how people trouble and struggle about these things and what dreadful persons get them, I cannot understand it at all. You are too proud of your William to want him to be anything else or to wear stars.' Four great dances a year were held at Sandringham, including one for Alix's birthday. The princess's lameness did not prevent her joining in with gusto, nor did it stop her participating in games such as tennis, bowling, golf, and, in winter, skating. One of her favourite hobbies was photography, which she had taken up after being given a camera by Queen Victoria.

The art was relatively unsophisticated at this time, but Alix took photographs of her family which survive.

Over the years, she became reconciled with the queen, whose attitude towards her daughter-in-law had always been fickle. Victoria was touched by the concern Alix showed over the death of her devoted servant, John Brown, an event ignored by the rest of the family. 'Nothing could exceed her tender sympathy and complete understanding of all I feel and suffer.' The queen told a visitor to Balmoral:

> For many years the princess has tried to spare me the strain and fatigue of functions . . . However terrible the load which I lay upon her slender shoulders, she not only never complains, but endeavours to prove that she had enjoyed what to another would be a tiresome duty . . . I am gratified to feel secure that, when I am no more, a Queen of England worthy of England's throne will give it grace.

(It is worth noting that even the queen made the mistake of using the name of 'England' to refer to the whole of her kingdom.)

The Princess of Wales was unquestionably the most popular member of the royal family, even among the working classes and anti-monarchist sympathizers. When she and her husband visited a factory in Manchester, Alexandra was allowed to try out the electroplating process. Shortly afterwards, a *Punch* cartoon showed her cutting short the claws of the 'Republican lion'. Another magazine, in 1890, published a satirical poem, in which she was the only one of the royals not held up to ridicule, the author saying:

> Your every word, your every glance
> Is able to the land entrance.

It was with the medical profession that this Princess of Wales would be most closely associated in later life. Her interest began with the fall of Khartoum in 1885. Alix founded a branch of a Danish charity for the aid of the war-wounded, aiming to ensure that it cared for servicemen in time of peace as well as war. She followed up that project by supporting the London Hospital, and the culmination of her efforts was Queen Alexandra's Imperial Military Nursing Service (the 'QAs').

Another triumph for her determination was the introduction into Britain of a device known as the Finsen lamp, invented by a Danish doctor to treat patients with lupus, a disease of the auto-immune system affecting the skin. One of many who benefited from Alexandra's devotion to the needs of others was John Merrick, known to history as the 'Elephant Man'. The Princess of Wales, hearing of his plight, insisted on visiting him in the London Hospital, where many of the nurses could not bear to look at him. She sent him a card and present every Christmas, and he treasured her photograph.

It was well known that the Prince of Wales still had affairs with women such as the actress, Lillie Langtry, and afterwards with Lady Brooke. While she was in Russia, rumours reached Alix that trouble was brewing over Lady Brooke's relationship with Lord Charles Beresford, an old friend of the prince. Bertie was simultaneously called to give evidence in the prosecution of an acquaintance for slander resulting from illegal gambling activities. At the age of fifty and a grandfather, he was still a play-boy at heart, and his wife had little alternative but to maintain a dignified silence. We might ask whether it was any easier for Alix, with her breeding and knowledge of what was expected of her, to accept his adultery than it would have been for another woman, or whether she felt the indignation a betrayed woman would feel nowadays. 'The babbling Brooke', later Countess of Warwick, was the only one of the prince's mistresses that the princess absolutely refused to tolerate.

What caused Alix to cut short her Russian trip was not her husband's fiftieth birthday party, nor his misbehaviour, but the news that her younger son, George, was suffering from typhoid, the disease that had killed his grandfather and almost killed his father. His constitution was strong, and he recovered, but only months later, his elder brother, Eddy, the Duke of Clarence, died of influenza. Eddy was in many ways his mother's favourite, and took more after her side of the family than his surviving brother. He was also due to be married.

The suddenness of Eddy's death was an enormous shock to his parents. His fiancée, Princess May of Teck, later said that, when Eddy's mother realized death was inevitable, 'the despairing look on her face was the most heart-rending thing I have ever seen'. Alix pined for him and insisted on his room being kept just as he had left it. On his seat in Sandringham church she had a plaque installed which read: 'This place was occupied for twenty-eight years by my darling Eddy, next to his ever sorrowing and loving Mother dear.' The family's spirits were raised a little when Eddy's fiancée agreed to an engagement with Prince George. May would be Princess of Wales after all. There was a parallel within Alexandra's own family, since her sister, having gone to Russia for the purpose of marrying Grand Duke Nicholas, had, following his death, married his younger brother instead.

A year after Eddy's death, personal unhappiness resurfaced for the Princess of Wales, when her faithful friend Oliver Montagu died aged only forty-eight. The princess was said to have cried non-stop for three days. This might simply have reflected her tender-heartedness, but it's more likely that her feelings for Montagu were deeper than mere friendship demanded. Somehow, Alix pulled herself together and assumed a brave public face.

Soon she was a grandmother again, when May gave birth to a son in 1894. He was called David, but he would, briefly, become King Edward VIII. The Prince and Princess of Wales continued to travel Europe on behalf of Queen Victoria, and these were dangerous times. Violence in Greece and Russia threatened the princess's brother and sister. While they were en route to Denmark in 1900, an anarchist fired a pistol at Alix and Bertie as they sat in their rail carriage in Brussels. The danger was real, and on their safe return to Britain the couple were rapturously received, for the old queen was near death. In January 1901, with Alix at her bedside, Victoria died.

At the funeral, Bertie's daughter-in-law, Princess May, was heard to exclaim, 'God help us all', and she was not the only one with doubts as to the new king's abilities. As a monarch, Edward VII did a better job than anyone expected, revealing an enlightened and progressive mind and a genuine concern for his subjects' welfare. Whatever his faults, he was loved both by his own family and by the nation, who regarded him as a breath of fresh air after his mother's seemingly endless reign.

Alix saw no particular difference in the role of a queen consort from that of an absolute monarch. She had not relished taking on the role, but she enjoyed the freedom and privilege that her new position gave her. She shrugged off advice about the coronation, saying: 'I know better than all the milliners and antiquaries. I shall wear exactly what I like.' In terms of stately elegance she far outshone her predecessor, but her human side was also more apparent than Victoria's had been. Perhaps for this reason, her husband did not confide in her about affairs of state. A lady-in-waiting wrote that she 'had the faculty of skimming easily over the surface of life and ignoring things which she disliked'.

The new king and queen moved into Buckingham Palace, which Alix delighted in redecorating in a more contemporary style. Windsor Castle also received a makeover. Of the other royal homes, she did not care for Balmoral or for Osborne House. The latter was given to the nation.

Queen Alexandra's chief contribution to British life in her later years was as a patron of various charities. The coronation had been delayed for two months because the king was dangerously ill with appendicitis, and Alix had to be dissuaded by the surgeon from witnessing the life-saving operation. She celebrated his recovery with an enormous banquet for the poor of London. The king, too, was active in charity work; he founded a major hospital fund in 1897. To these good causes, Alix added a personal touch. She attended the sick in Sandringham village, and nursed her own maid when she fell fatally ill. In his 1992 biography of the royal couple, Richard Hough writes that 'she had that rare talent for personal communication which made each patient feel picked out for special sympathy'. He leaves unstated the parallel with another Princess of Wales.

At the coronation, Queen Alexandra almost outshone her husband, in a dress of Indian gauze with elaborate gold embroidery and a train of purple velvet. Her jewels included the Dagmar Cross. The Koh-i-noor diamond, inherited from her mother-in-law, Queen Victoria, had been set into a crown. Flanked by two bishops, the queen preceded the king into Westminster Abbey, attended by four duchesses whose role was to hold the canopy while she was crowned. Lady Jane Lindsay was one of those who observed the ceremony: 'Words fail to say how marvellous she looked, moving down with her crown glittering with diamonds, a sceptre in each hand.'

The new queen's ability to maintain her appearance was remarkable. In 1906, when Alix was sixty-two, the Princess of Pless described her as follows: 'She does not look a day over fifty, and has a lovely figure and a straight back, and fresh red lips that are not painted . . . I have seen her at Cowes in the pouring rain, and she is certainly not enamelled.' The characteristic collar-style necklaces which were so admired had, ironically, begun as a way of disguising a scar on her neck.

Even as king, Bertie remained interested in women other than his stunning wife. His long-standing mistress, Alice Keppel, was tolerated by Alix, because of her personal charm and discretion. Mrs Keppel received gifts from the new queen, and was allowed to take an annual holiday alone in the king's company. Alix still refused to stand for Daisy, Lady Warwick, and insisted that her liaison with the king be brought to an end.

Relations with both France and Germany were strained during the reign of Edward VII. His nephew, Kaiser Wilhelm II, was difficult to get along with, and war was being predicted long before it actually happened. For Alix, this came as no surprise, as she had an obsessional hatred for everything German, and had refused to allow her eldest son to contemplate marrying one of Wilhelm's sisters. When her other son, George, received an honorary colonel's rank in a Prussian regiment, she remarked: 'It is your misfortune, not your fault.' Fortunately Alix played little part in diplomatic missions; when she travelled as queen, it was to destinations where she had family, such as Denmark and Russia.

The king and queen liked to travel incognito. In 1907, they went for a private holiday to Paris, travelling under the pseudonym of the Duke and Duchess of Lancaster. They stayed at the British Embassy, and tried to behave like a normal couple seeing the sights. The French press went wild over Alix, but the Germans were incensed at the increasing *entente cordiale* between Britain and France. In an attempt to soothe them, the king invited Kaiser Wilhelm to visit Britain, and Alix was forced to overcome her dislike and welcome him.

The following year, despite the king's rapidly-failing health, he and his queen travelled together to Scandinavia, meeting the tsar of Russia aboard the royal yacht. Determined to maintain peaceful relations with Germany, they went to Berlin in 1909 to visit the Kaiser, though neither of them now felt up to travelling.

The visit was fraught with incident, and the king collapsed during a state banquet. Although he recovered, it was obvious that his days were numbered, and he was rumoured to be considering abdication in favour of the Prince of Wales. At home, there was another political crisis; but, during the summer, he holidayed in Europe, and his popularity reached its peak when his horse won the Derby.

Despite his age and general ill health, Bertie's death in 1910 came quite suddenly. The queen returned from Corfu, where she had been visiting her brother, to find him suffering from bronchitis, and his final collapse came shortly afterwards. She remained with him throughout his illness, administering the oxygen he needed as he struggled with death. Alix described herself as 'turned to stone' by the loss of her lifelong companion, unable to cry or make any fuss, but continuing to go about her duties without understanding what she was doing. They had been married for forty-seven years.

Bertie's funeral was one of the last and greatest gatherings of crowned heads of Europe. Seven kings were present, including the kaiser. Departing from tradition, Alix took precedence over the new queen, Mary, and made sure that Bertie's beloved dog, Caesar, walked behind the coffin. As queen mother, Alix would lose many of the privileges she had enjoyed as queen. She was able to stay at Sandringham, the home she had acquired early in her married life, but her London home was no longer Buckingham Palace. She found it no great hardship to return to Marlborough House.

Family deaths and tragedies continued to be faced at intervals. The worst shock was the murder of Alix's brother, King George of Greece, at Salonika in 1913. The same year should have been her fiftieth wedding anniversary. To commemorate the occasion, she began a new charity event, the Alexandra Rose Day. It was patronized by the military leader Lord Kitchener, whose legendary misogyny seemed to disappear in her presence. Having come to terms with no longer being first lady, she was comfortable with a retreat to Sandringham when the First World War broke out in 1914. The retired Admiral 'Jackie' Fisher, a great friend of both Alix and Bertie, became First Sea Lord in his seventies following the forced resignation of Prince Louis of Battenberg, and this enabled the queen mother to keep in touch with events.

The Russian Revolution of 1917, followed by the assassination of the royal family, was another major blow, but Alix's sister, Minnie, managed to escape, rescued from Yalta by a British cruiser sent on the express orders of King George V. The two sisters continued to see one another in their declining years. Alix's deafness increased, and her eyesight began to fail. It became an effort to maintain her personal standards of dress and appearance. One of her last public engagements was the wedding of her grandson, the Duke of York, to Lady Elizabeth Bowes-Lyon, on 26 April 1923. She was well enough to pose for a photograph with her son King George V, his daughter the Princess Royal, and Alix's great-grandson, George Lascelles; but shortly afterwards she made her last Alexandra Rose Day drive, and she was no longer able to enjoy life as she had done. The special film made for her eightieth birthday, to be shown in cinemas, was accompanied by this tribute from *The Times*: 'When Hans Andersen used to tell the little Princess Alexandra his immortal stories, he fostered in her ardent childish imagination his own conception of a living and loving fairyland brought down on earth, a gracious, healing influence on ordinary human joys and sorrows.'

Others were not slow in coming forward with similar compliments. 'She gives to everyone who asks; she cannot refuse', said Lord Knutsford, head of the London Hospital. 'There are not many people in Queen Alexandra's position who would have taken an eight-mile drive in an open cart on a stormy and rainy April afternoon in order to avoid disappointing a dying child', agreed Lord Frederic Hamilton. George Dangerfield remarked on her 'instinctive kindness and an almost childlike zest for life'. None of her predecessors as Princess of Wales had lived to a comparable age, or had such a successful career either as princess or queen. It was her successor as both, Queen Mary, who was holding Alexandra's hand when she passed away in 1925.

Any assessment of Alexandra's contribution as Princess of Wales must inevitably concentrate on her humanity and compassion, attributes which had not been notable in the royal family, even its female members, over the centuries. She brought to her position as second lady of the land a personal style that was almost unknown and would not be known again until the

Opening of the Alexandra Dock in Cardiff, 1907.
A photograph taken by Alexandra as queen.

late twentieth century. It was at Sandringham that her loss was most keenly felt. She was, as none of her predecessors as Princess of Wales had been, a people's princess. She was also, despite living into the twentieth century, married to a man who did not always treat her with the respect due to a wife. Had she lived in the present day, regardless of her position as Princess of Wales and later queen, no reasonable person would have expected her to tolerate his behaviour.

Mary of Teck (1867–1953)

Alexandra's immediate successor, Princess Mary (or 'May') of Teck, like some of her forerunners, became Princess of Wales after the husband originally earmarked for her had died an untimely death. Once again, we find a Princess of Wales being passed on from one prospective king to another in order to fulfil her destiny.

The Duke of Clarence, known as Prince 'Eddy', was never a good advertisement for the royal family, having something of his father's youthful character. So reckless was his lifestyle that one vicious rumour identified him with the elusive murderer Jack the Ripper. He drank heavily, and his friendships with homosexuals were well known. When he was old enough to consider marriage, Eddy had caused his family enormous concern by selecting the daughter of a French count. Marriage to a Roman Catholic was forbidden for a member of the royal family, and Eddy would have lost his place in the line of succession if Hélène refused to renounce her faith. His parents, especially Alexandra, believing that marriage would steady him, tried in vain to achieve a compromise; in the end, the prince was left with no option but to find a suitable substitute.

May was the daughter of the Duke of Teck, an impoverished German nobleman, and of Princess Mary Adelaide, a cousin of Queen Victoria. Born in May 1867 at Kensington Palace, May was more English than any other nationality. Directly descended from George III, she was a cousin of the royal princes and had known them from youth. Her childhood had not been the happiest, her family being deeply in debt, something she had in common with Alexandra before her. Her other outstanding virtue in the eyes of the Princess of Wales was the same quality

*Mary of Teck, Duchess of York and later Princess of Wales, shortly
after her marriage to the future King George V.
From a Victorian print.*

Caroline of Ansbach had once recognized in the young Augusta of Saxe-Gotha: she was unlikely to outshine her mother-in-law.

May's own mother, nicknamed 'Fat Mary' because of her seventeen-stone figure, was known for her extravagance, and her fashion-consciousness would be inherited by her eldest daughter, so much so that Mary junior kept a written record of what she wore on special occasions. By the time of her engagement, her family were resident at White Lodge in Richmond Park, another home they owed to the kindness of the queen. Years later, May's first child would be born there. The house became part of the Royal Ballet School.

In her youth, May did not have great marital prospects. Her engagement to Prince Eddy came about within a short time of the break-up of his previous romance, and was carefully planned by both sets of parents. The prince had already been turned down by Princess Alix of Hesse, the ill-fated future tsarina of Russia. His parents were rightly doubtful about his ability to find a suitable wife without assistance. May admitted to her mother that she was not keen on the marriage. She had heard rumours about Eddy's rakish conduct, but was not brave enough to reject him. Had she only known it, he was, whilst courting her, looking twice at an earl's daughter. Eddy's family, seeing him on course to become a total disaster as king, sought a young woman who would keep him on the straight and narrow. Having been given the once-over by Queen Victoria at Balmoral, May was invited to the home of the Danish ambassador, to meet the prince 'officially'. Once she had accepted him, May found that she was expected to act as a kind of nursemaid-cum-secretary to her hopeless fiancé.

Queen Victoria was pleased with the choice of bride, as illustrated by one of her letters:

> People here are delighted and certainly she is a dear, good and clever girl, very carefully brought up, unselfish and unfrivolous in her tastes. She will be a great help to him. She is very fond of Germany too and is very cosmopolitan. I must say that I think it is far preferable than *eine kleine deutsche Prinzessin* [a little German princess] with no knowledge of anything beyond small German courts etc. It would never do for Eddy.

The Queen was writing in the expectation that Eddy would, on her death, become Prince of Wales and heir apparent. The reference to 'small German courts' is interesting when we consider past disasters such as that of Caroline of Brunswick, who had still been living when Victoria was born, and her indiscretions still fresh in the memory. Victoria was delighted to note that her new granddaughter-in-law 'has no frivolous tastes, has been very carefully brought up and is very well informed'. Mary's future father-in-law was equally approving. Speaking at a dinner towards the end of 1891, Bertie expressed pride that 'my son marries one who was born in this country, and has the feelings of an Englishwoman'. We can only wonder what the Prince of Wales would have said if his son had proposed to marry a Welshwoman!

The wedding was due to take place in February 1892, but first came Eddy's birthday party at Sandringham on 8 January. His sisters Victoria and Maud were suffering from influenza, an illness that was rife in the country at the time, and his younger brother George was recovering from typhoid. There was tension between the Prince and Princess of Wales, and the latter had been holidaying in Europe rather than attending her husband's birthday celebrations in the autumn. Naturally, she was at Sandringham to welcome the guests for her eldest son's birthday.

On the day before the party, the prince was taken ill. The party went ahead without him, as his illness did not seem to be serious, but he contracted pneumonia and died a week later, with his mother and fiancée at his bedside.

May's mother later described her 'dazed misery'. Her true feelings must have been mixed. For one thing, Eddy, when delirious, had been heard to call out for Hélène. To a friend, May wrote that it was 'difficult to begin one's old life again after such a shock . . . I cannot settle down to anything.' It would have been only human of her to have felt a slight sense of relief. Eddy's death came as a bigger blow to her parents, who had been counting on the marriage to reverse their fortunes.

It was less common in those days for the public to be enlightened by the newspapers as to the 'truth' behind events involving the royal family, however vital to the future of the nation. A popular ballad claimed to reflect public feeling:

> A nation wrapped in mourning
> Sheds bitter tears today,
> For the noble Duke of Clarence
> And fair young Princess May.

Tennyson, still active as Poet Laureate, was inspired by the sight of May placing a garland of orange blossom on Eddy's coffin during the funeral service.

For the Tecks, all was not lost. May had, naturally, become popular during her brief engagement to the heir to the throne, and was now encouraged to marry his younger brother, George, who would be the next Prince of Wales. His bereaved parents had become fond of May, and insisted on giving her the wedding presents that had been intended for her as Eddy's wife. George, though a steadier character than his elder brother, had not been without romantic entanglements. Wild rumours circulated that he had secretly married the daughter of an admiral in Malta, and these were repeated years later, after he became king. There was absolutely no truth in them; he had barely met the woman in question, which merely goes to show that the conduct of the press has not changed as much over the years as we might think.

At the time of his brother's death, George held no title, but he was made Duke of York later in the year. Though the two brothers had been close, George had a quite different personality from Eddy, more disciplined and more intelligent (though not outstandingly bright). May could almost have been said to have struck lucky. The old queen, who held such strong opinions on the suitability of royal marriages, had already approved May as a potential future queen, which in itself sheds light on the girl's personality. George, however, had been and probably still was in love with a cousin, Princess Marie of Edinburgh. Marie had been married off to the crown prince of Romania, and it took a little time for the disappointed suitor to be persuaded to take the diplomatic course. True to form, he soon transferred his affections sincerely and wholeheartedly. Exactly a year after her engagement to Prince Eddy, May met George again at Sandringham, and a few months later he proposed to her in the garden at White Lodge. They married in July 1893, eighteen months after Eddy's death, at the Chapel Royal in St James's Palace.

A letter George wrote years later sums up their relationship: 'People say I only married you out of pity and sympathy. That shows how little the world really knows what it is talking about.' Likewise, May's letters to George disprove the idea that she was not in love with George, but wanted only the prestige and position he gave her. 'I am very sorry that I am still so shy with you . . . I love you more than anybody in the world, and this I cannot tell you myself so I write it to relieve my feelings.'

Royal weddings were already big business, and the public was treated to special editions of popular magazines and newspapers, an exhibition of wedding presents and a series of events leading up to the wedding day at which the young couple, especially the bride, were on display. It was a national holiday, and the ceremony was attended by several European royals.

The Princess of Wales had begun to show signs of jealousy at the marriage of her second son, to whom she had transferred all the affection previously reserved for Eddy. Queen Victoria, however, wrote in her diary: 'Dear May looked so pretty and quiet and dignified.' A more censorious wedding guest compared the bride unfavourably with her mother-in-law. 'Instead of coming in the exquisite, ideal way the Princess of Wales did at her wedding with her eyes cast down – so prettily – May looked right and left and slightly bowed to her acquaintance! A great mistake.'

The couple honeymooned at Sandringham, taking up residence in the tiny York Cottage (now the Sandringham estate manager's office). In London, their home would be York House, a wing of St James's Palace. Almost immediately upon her marriage, May began the education of her husband, illustrating the character of a woman who, having been forced to marry appropriately, set out to see that her husband lived up to her own and everyone else's expectations. For her, the titles of Duke and Duchess of York, which would in due course give way to those of Prince and Princess of Wales, were mere stepping stones on the way to the throne.

Their first child, named Edward but always familiarly known by his last Christian name of David, was born the following year. He was destined to be Prince of Wales and, briefly, king. A second son, Albert George, also to be king, came along the year after that, on the anniversary of the death of his great-grand-father, Prince Albert. Queen Victoria commented that 'he could hardly have been called by any other name', and he was always known at home as 'Bertie', though as king he would take the title of George VI. The children's mother found pregnancy and childbirth 'distasteful', and carried on producing offspring only from a sense of duty. Her children were brought up by nannies, not always with the best results. May said that her eldest son was 'exactly what I looked like as a baby, consequently *plain*. This is a pity and rather disturbs me.' A strange comment from a new mother.

George and May were strict parents, but George was feared more by the children. David once commented that 'We used to have a most lovely time with her alone – always laughing and joking . . . She was a different human being away from him.' Their married life was quite unlike that of the Prince and Princess of Wales, George's parents, and the difference was not accidental. May disapproved of horse racing and gambling, favourite pastimes of her mother-in-law as well as her father-in-law, and supported her husband's determination not to slip into the ways that had damaged his father's reputation. May and George preferred to be at home together, though they were much in demand socially. May also disliked her father-in-law's philandering; she sympathized with 'Motherdear'.

Though May was a conventional young woman, she managed, like so many princesses before and after her, to be a leader of fashion. In her youth, she took to wearing a hairpiece attached to the front of her head to give a kind of curly fringe, which was not always favourably commented on. One of her favourite garments was the small shoulder cape, and she also wore hats called 'toques' that were admired and copied, even though they made her appear taller than her husband (which she was). She would retain roughly the same style of dress into her old age. It became her practice to obtain her outfits from leading British designers, at a knock-down price reflecting the value of the free advertising to them.

If anything, May and George were adopting a way of life more like that of his grandparents than that of his parents. Victoria encouraged May to call her 'Grandmama'. She approved of May, whereas Alexandra found her new daughter-in-law rather staid. She was certainly not the vivacious beauty that Alix had been in her youth; yet she had a desire to please that stood her in good stead when the pressure of royal life became apparent. May prided herself on never complaining about any aspect of public duty. Victoria wrote to her in 1897: 'Each time I see you, I love and respect you more and am so truly thankful that Georgie has such a partner.'

In that same year, shortly after taking part in the queen's Diamond Jubilee celebrations, Princess Mary Adelaide died. The loss of her mother was deeply felt by May, but she kept her feelings in check, unlike Princess Alexandra, who is said to have cried loudest of all at the funeral. May's father went into a mental decline from which he never recovered. May soon stopped visiting him because of the upset it caused. She had other preoccupations, in the form of more children. The couple's first and only daughter, diplomatically named Victoria Alexandra Alice Mary, was born at Sandringham in April, 1897. Henry, Duke of Gloucester, came along in March 1900. George, Duke of Kent, was their last healthy son; he arrived in December 1902.

Shortly after Victoria's death, the newly promoted Prince and Princess of Wales moved into Marlborough House, vacated by May's in-laws in favour of Buckingham Palace. Her own position was elevated to that of the second most important woman in the country, and she conducted herself accordingly. Alix was anxious that her son and his wife should not assume their new titles too quickly, claiming that it would confuse the public.

The couple and their four children continued to spend family time at York Cottage, under the eye of the king and queen at Sandringham. The new king respected his daughter-in-law, who, he saw, was bright enough to be of great practical help to George in the future; his own wife was not considered fitted to participate in affairs of state. A well-known story relates how the king informed the Prince of Wales that he would be allowed to see all the official papers in future and he should also show them to May. George, surprised, protested, 'But Mother doesn't see them.' The king replied, 'No, but that's a very different thing.'

One of the first official duties of the Prince and Princess of Wales in their new role was to undertake a tour of the Commonwealth (still the Empire at that time), planned before the death of the old queen. The children were left at home, to be looked after by their grandmother, Queen Alexandra, whose style of child-rearing differed considerably from that of her daughter-in-law. May was not without feeling for her family, and cried in her cabin as the ship left Portsmouth. To make matters worse, the princess was sick for most of her time at sea. Despite these sufferings and although May was not exactly an extrovert, the tour was much more of a personal triumph for her than for her husband, who found it difficult to make an impact. They returned to Britain to find their younger children much changed; even their older sons were nervous of seeing them again. Around this time, Bertie, their second son, developed a stutter that plagued him for the rest of his life.

The official investiture of May and her husband as Prince and Princess of Wales took place in November 1901, on the king's sixtieth birthday. George also succeeded his father as chancellor of the University of Wales, an unsuitable role for one so academically unremarkable. Changes to their household included the addition of the Countess of Airlie, May's friend, as one of her new ladies-in-waiting. She arrived on St David's Day (a date that seems to have held no particular significance for the household), and recorded her observations on the subject in her memoirs.

The princess had not yet fully adjusted to her new role. The king was still referred to as 'Uncle Wales', and his sudden illness, which caused the postponement of the coronation, threw the family into a panic. The new Prince of Wales dreaded the prospect, however distant, of becoming king, despite his disciplined lifestyle and devotion to duty. This crisis caused George and May to begin grooming their eldest son, David, at an early age for his future role as monarch.

Tension grew between May and Alix. When the Princess of Wales had to stand in for the queen at court, Alix refused to allow her own ladies-in-waiting to attend her daughter-in-law. May would not allow herself to be trampled on. At the same time as becoming Princess of Wales, she had assumed the role of head of the Teck family. Her younger brother, Frank, was a constant trial, and the king's help had to be enlisted to sort out his financial (and other) affairs.

More travelling on behalf of the king was soon required. Once again, the children were left with their grandparents. May, who had not lived a sheltered life, was appalled by the position of women in India, and instructed her husband to raise the issue whenever the opportunity arose. In Spain, an anarchist threw a bomb in the street and killed twenty onlookers. In all this period, the princess's contact with her children was of a formal nature. Soon David was sent away to the Royal Naval College at Queen Victoria's old home, Osborne on the Isle of Wight. Bertie followed. Both were following in their father's footsteps, but neither had a truly kingly disposition.

The two boys would be hard hit by the death of their grandfather, Edward VII, in 1910. Even more deeply affected was Queen Alexandra, who clung to her position. May's comments about her mother-in-law at this time are sharp, but opinions vary as to which, if either, of the two women found it harder to compromise. They had very different personalities.

Edward VII, once he succeeded his mother, was determined that his son and heir should be fully involved in the business of ruling the country, in a way that Queen Victoria had never allowed him to be, and he extended this involvement to his daughter-in-law. It is clear, however, that the Princess of Wales's own interests and abilities were subsumed by her husband's. Mary came into her own only after George's death, when as queen mother she had an important role to play in the abdication crisis of 1936, living on through the Second World War, when British people were glad of the example set by the royal family. In this role, she is clearly remembered by many British people today.

Throughout her time as Princess of Wales, Mary had maintained relationships with old friends on the Continent, including her aunt, Grand Duchess Augusta. As late as 1913, May and George were making a personal visit to Germany, but relations were shortly to be severed by the First World War (though Mary continued to receive letters from the grand duchess until Augusta's death in 1916). Even in these times, anti-German feeling was apparently fostered more by Queen Alexandra than by the young king and queen. During the war, the official name of the British royal family was changed to Windsor, a public relations exercise cutting off any implicit connections with the German enemy.

Mary could not be said to have the common touch. Part of this was due to her natural reserve, which some would call shyness. The only time the general public had the opportunity to hear her voice was when the launch of the new Cunard liner, named *Queen Mary* in her honour, was broadcast on the wireless. Extremely conscious of her position and duties, she thought of ordinary people as the king's subjects, but not without affection. In the first year of the Great War, she had the brainwave of sending a Christmas gift to all those serving at the front. She insisted that her family make suitable sacrifices to show solidarity with the people's suffering, and encouraged her daughter to become a student nurse. The queen visited the wounded in hospital, though she hated the sight of blood.

In the course of her marriage she had given birth to six children, but her attitude to them was more like that of the Hanoverian queens than that of her mother-in-law, Alexandra. Her excuse was that 'their father is also their king'. She was unaware that the nurse appointed to look after her sons was ill-treating them, until it was brought to the family's attention by another member of the royal household. Her only daughter, the Princess Royal, named Mary after her mother, was the child who most resembled her mother in character. The youngest son, John, mentally retarded and an epileptic, was kept out of the public eye until his early death; this was for his own good, but reflects his mother's view of the importance of outward appearances for the monarchy. No wonder she later found her eldest son's decision to marry Wallis Simpson and abdicate the throne impossible either to understand or to forgive.

By the time of the abdication crisis, Mary was not only a mother but a grandmother, and she seems to have had a better relationship with her grandchildren and great-grandchildren than she ever did with her children. Whilst eager to dictate how their parents brought them up, she showed more affection and tolerance than she had done as a young mother. In private, she certainly had a sense of humour; if anything it was her husband who was the more strait-laced. Popular references to 'George and the Dragon' were quite unfair. Aspects of Mary's behaviour have their roots in her upbringing, but she was undeniably old-fashioned. Even before she married into the royal family, she is reported to have scoffed at the way Alexandra continued to hold birthday parties for her children in their late teens. It was often remarked that the reign of George V more resembled his grandmother's than that of his father.

In 1911 the new king and queen were crowned emperor and empress of India at Delhi in an opulent ceremony. This followed a rather different kind of ceremony that had taken place earlier in the year.

Three weeks after the coronation of the king and queen at Westminster in 1911, the time came to invest the heir to the throne with the title of Prince of Wales, at a ceremony held in Wales itself. The chancellor of the exchequer, David Lloyd George, was MP for Caernarfon and an enthusiastic Welsh-speaking patriot. It was at his instigation that the king agreed to the revolutionary idea of holding the investiture in the very place where the title had traditionally been first given to the son of an English king. (Curiously, the mayor of Chester tried to make a case for holding the ceremony there, on the grounds that one of the prince's titles was Earl of Chester!)

David would be the first 'English' Prince of Wales to be invested with his title at a ceremony held within his principality. The idea had originated from the bishop of St Asaph (later the first archbishop of Wales), who thought it would heal divisions as well as bringing Wales a higher profile. There had been much industrial strife, and the question of disestablishment of the Church in Wales was under discussion. Such an elaborate investiture ceremony had last been performed under James I, and never in this location. Work had to be done on the castle. The walls were repaired using stone from the original quarries, owned by the Marquess of Anglesey. To receive the traditional insignia of the Prince of Wales, a gold rod, a gold ring, a coronet and a sword, the Prince wore what he called a 'preposterous rig' of white satin breeches, a coronet and a robe trimmed with ermine. He carried a sword and sceptre and nearly fainted in the heat of the July day.

Not everyone in Wales was in favour of the investiture. A nationalist movement was beginning to make its presence felt. The Scotsman, Keir Hardie, elected for Merthyr as the first-ever Labour MP some years earlier, declared the occasion to be 'a reminder that an English King and his robber barons strove for ages to destroy the Welsh people, and finally succeeded in robbing them of their lands . . . The ceremony ought to make every Welshman who is a patriot blush with shame.'

Mary was of course present at Caernarfon, travelling to the castle by carriage with the king, their daughter and the Duke of Connaught, last surviving son of Queen Victoria. They were received by the mayor and the prime minister. Speeches were made and hymns sung in English and Welsh, and those attending the ceremony were reminded in the king's speech that the new prince had Tudor ancestry.

The queen later wrote that her seventeen-year-old son had 'looked charming' and 'did his part very well'. (Faint praise from a mother, one might think.) His 'part' included a few halting sentences in the Welsh language, taught to the prince by Lloyd George. Ironically, David's parents disliked the Welshman, who was to take advantage of the king's political naïveté on more than one occasion. We may surmise from her words that the ceremony and the title of Prince of Wales had only a superficial meaning for David's mother, despite the fact that she had herself been Princess of Wales. The new prince, by his famous visit to the south Wales mining communities, would later show that he had a better appreciation of its significance, but he never fulfilled his promise. After less than a year on the throne, he would abdicate in order to marry a twice-divorced American, and even his mother would be unable to dissuade him.

In 1912 a strike of coal miners and factory workers almost brought the country to a standstill. It was prompted by the campaign for a minimum wage of five shillings a day, and the king had little influence over the actions taken by Parliament to address the problem. Both he and the queen were distressed by it; 'if only one could act . . .', said Mary. On hearing that the royal couple proposed to visit Dowlais ironworks, Keir Hardie made his views known, once again, by writing an open letter to his monarch, published in the *Merthyr Pioneer*. 'From a people so kindly as the Welsh,' said Hardie, 'you are bound . . . to receive a warm welcome, but that warmth will be turned to enthusiasm if you boldly take your stand on the side of the workers . . .'

The king and queen, contrary to popular expectation, were sympathetic to the conditions in which working people lived. They visited some of the worst-affected areas, and Queen Mary even went to tea at the home of a south Wales miner. Privately, however, she remarked to her husband that the government was to blame for the crisis because of 'their extraordinary tactics in encouraging socialism all these years and in pandering to the Labour Party'. She was no egalitarian.

The outbreak of war forced the nation to pull together. The king had tried to maintain good relations with Germany, through his cousin, the Kaiser, but now his sons faced active service, David with the army and Bertie with the navy. As heir to the throne, David was effectively kept away from the front – a great frustration for him – but Bertie was involved in naval battles, and made a successful career for himself in the navy. In 1918 news of the assassination of the entire Russian royal family, close relations of the Windsors, reached Britain, adding to the heartache of the king and queen. Yet, when the war ended, Queen Mary showed no particular eagerness for the return of her sons, writing only: 'I think David ought to return home before very long, as he must help us in these difficult days.'

The young Prince of Wales was immensely popular, and had begun to take a more public role. His friendship with a married woman, Freda Dudley Ward, was causing his parents concern. His bachelor apartment at York House was the setting for intimate meetings with Mrs Dudley Ward, but in public he was the life and soul of every party, and associated rather too closely with ordinary people for his parents' liking. His mother suggested an official visit to India as a solution to the problem.

Shortly after the war, Prince John died, aged thirteen. Because of his physical and mental shortcomings, John had been placed in a country retreat, though his existence was hardly the secret suggested by television dramatists. Deeply upset, Mary wrote stoically to a friend that she was grateful he had been spared further deterioration. As usual, Queen Alexandra showed far more sign of outward grief. Suitable marriage partners were now being sought for some of the older children. The Princess Royal had received a proposal from Viscount Lascelles, who was some years older than her but acceptable to her parents. The Prince of Wales looked unlikely to settle down for some time yet.

The queen had spotted a suitable wife for her second son, Bertie. Lady Elizabeth Bowes-Lyon, daughter of the Earl of Strathmore, would be one of her successors as queen, but in the early 1920s, Mary encouraged her presence only because she felt she was 'the one girl who could make Bertie happy'. Uncharacteristically, she determined not to interfere. Eventually, it was through her friend, the Countess of Airlie, that she helped bring the young couple together. Both this royal wedding and that of the Princess Royal were made much fuss of by the press and helped increase the popularity of the royal family.

Another notable event in Queen Mary's career was her participation in the project to build a doll's house with the intention of displaying the best of craftsmanship in miniature, leaving an example for future generations of the royal lifestyle in the 1920s. Designed by Sir Edwin Lutyens, Queen Mary's Dolls' House is still on show at Windsor.

In 1928, by which time he was a grandfather several times over, George V was taken seriously ill, and the Prince of Wales was recalled from a visit to Africa. The king was suffering from septicaemia, and needed emergency surgery. He convalesced at Bognor Regis, where the queen, despite her dislike of illness in general, accompanied him. The Prince of Wales was by now in his thirties, and the nation was becoming impatient for him to marry, a situation that would repeat itself fifty years later. His younger brother, George, Duke of Kent, was soon to marry the Greek Princess Marina, who would become a great favourite of the British public, and his other brother, Henry, Duke of Gloucester, soon married.

David's flirtation with an American, Thelma, Lady Furness, led to his being introduced to another American, the divorcée Wallis Simpson, a strange mixture of sophistication and vulgarity whose appeal was to last. When the queen learned of their affair, she chose to overlook it, failing to recognize that Mrs Simpson, like herself, was a strong and determined woman and therefore more dangerous than the prince's previous mistresses. As a displacement activity to take her mind off the king's continuing poor health and her worries over her eldest son, Mary devised the idea of a Silver Jubilee celebration in 1935. After a procession through London and a service at St Paul's Cathedral, the king broadcast to the nation over the radio, including the queen in his thanks to his people.

George V was still deteriorating physically. His sister's sudden death at the end of 1935 was a shock, and he cancelled the state opening of Parliament for the first time in his reign. Another war with Germany was already predicted by some, and there was a general election to be arranged. By the middle of January, the king's death was imminent. Queen Mary, with typical understatement, wrote to the Prince of Wales that 'Papa is not very well' and suggested he be present at Sandringham for the end. She remained at the king's bedside almost continuously. Apparently her first action, when the end had come, was to take her son's hand and proclaim 'God save the King' to those present. In her diary that night, all she wrote was: 'Such a sad day.' Mary was evidently recalling the death of her husband's brother, Prince Eddy, nearly forty-five years earlier.

She returned to London on the royal train, with the king's coffin. An onlooker described her as 'erect and more magnificent than ever'. At each station on the way to Windsor, after the lying in state, crowds gathered to pay their last respects. Curiously, Mary seems to have felt a kind of relief at relinquishing her position and moving out of Buckingham Palace. Her worries were far from over, however, and she would not yet be able to forget her duty to the nation; she was still, nominally, the first lady of the land.

The new king's relationship with Mrs Simpson was a favourite topic with the American press; British newspapers carefully avoiding the subject for diplomatic reasons. (We cannot imagine such a situation nowadays.) Mrs Simpson had petitioned for divorce, and the king immediately informed the prime minister of his intention of marrying her. Unknown to him, the queen mother had already approached politicians to assess the situation and seek a solution. In his own memoirs, Edward VIII wrote: 'My mother had been schooled to put duty in the stoic Victorian sense before everything else in life.' He spoke envyingly of 'her invincible virtue and correctness'.

Shortly after a confrontation with his mother, in November 1936, the king visited Merthyr and Dowlais and made an off-the-cuff remark about the living and working conditions of the people which went down in Welsh history. 'Something should be done,' he said, to get people back to work. The comment embedded itself in the minds of those who heard it and caused the Welsh working class to hope for his assistance in their struggle against unemployment. The *Western Mail* published an open letter to the king, echoing the sentiments Keir Hardie had expressed twenty-five years earlier.

The king's good intentions took second place to his determination to marry Mrs Simpson, and the queen mother was faced with the task of dissuading her son from abdicating. Bertie, whose success as king had been foreseen by his late father, was immensely reluctant to take on the role. His mother displayed little outward sympathy for his predicament and urged him to do his duty, but she wrote in her own diary: 'It is a terrible blow to us all and particularly to poor Bertie.' To a friend, she remarked: 'He is the one who is making the sacrifice.' This sentiment was echoed in a letter she wrote to the ex-king some time after his abdication: 'It seemed inconceivable to those who had made such sacrifices during the war that you, as their King, refused a lesser sacrifice.'

Queen Mary lived on to see her second son, as George VI, bring the nation through another world war and restore the public respect for the monarchy which was so important to her. Her presence at his coronation in Westminster Abbey was a new departure for a queen mother, and there is no doubt that she did this with the idea of supporting him. The coronation proved that she was still exceptionally popular, as a huge cheer went up from the crowd when she arrived at the abbey, a symbol of continuity and stability. By now she was almost seventy. She confided in old friends how difficult it had been for her to see someone else take her place as queen, and she maintained her own 'court' at Marlborough House, where men were still forced to wear knee breeches.

Sandringham, the country home of Bertie and Alexandra and later of George and Mary. One of many photographs taken by the princess.

Though her eldest son, under the title of Duke of Windsor, was living in exile in France, Mary continued to correspond with him revealing true maternal feeling. 'Our being parted and the cause of it, grieve me beyond words,' she wrote; but she was emphatic about refusing to receive his wife.

She remained popular with the masses, and throughout the Second World War, she behaved in her customary majestic manner, whilst again showing her adaptability in the face of national emergency, though she did retire to Badminton House in Gloucestershire while the king and queen remained in London. They kept closely in touch, and in 1942 came the news that the Duke of Kent, Mary's youngest surviving son, had been killed on active service with the RAF. His wife, Marina, had given birth to her third child only a few weeks earlier. Once again, the queen mother displayed little outward emotion, but the loss helped bring the royal family yet closer to their people.

Victory over Germany was looking increasingly likely, and before long Mary was able to return to London and see her family more often. Lest we think of her as being completely lacking in a sense of fun, we may note that she particularly favoured Princess Elizabeth's younger sister, Margaret, whom she described as 'so outrageously amusing that one can't help but encourage her'. When, after the war, Elizabeth became engaged, her grandmother was delighted, and looked forward to the celebration of another royal wedding to lift the spirits of the British people.

Now eighty, Queen Mary was still corresponding with her eldest son, and the Duchess of Windsor engineered one last meeting between them. What Mary felt about his visit is uncertain, as she wrote nothing in her diary about it, but she took him with her to visit the East End and see the damage done by the blitz. It must have been a success, because he returned a few months later to see her again, vainly seeking some kind of official role on behalf of the British government abroad. It would be the last time mother and son met in private, and she continued to refuse to receive the Duchess of Windsor.

Great-grandchildren began arriving. Although Mary's health was failing, that of her son the king was worse, and Princess Elizabeth was being thrown into the spotlight. The king's death was a great blow to his mother, but she insisted on being the first to pay homage to the new queen when Elizabeth arrived back in London after hearing the news during an official visit to Africa. The Duke of Windsor, who saw his mother briefly on this occasion, commented on what he saw as her ability to bear a grudge: 'Mama as hard as nails,' he wrote, 'but fading.' As she watched her son's funeral procession from Marlborough House, the Countess of Airlie describes her as 'wrapped in the ineffable solitude of grief'.

When she died in 1953, two months before the coronation of her granddaughter, Queen Mary lay in state for three days at Westminster, arousing scenes of public grief and devotion in excess of anyone's expectations. She had already given instructions that the coronation was not to be postponed on her account. The announcement of her death was made in Parliament by the prime minister, Winston Churchill. Sir Henry Channon noted in his diary that 'There were cries of dismay from the Gallery, and indeed on all sides there seemed to be grief . . .

particularly from the Socialists. She had long captured their imagination, and they rightly thought her above politics.'

The Duke of Windsor, though not officially invited to the funeral, was present at the lying in state. The words he wrote to describe his feelings fail to reflect the close relationship he had had with her up to the time of his abdication: 'My sadness was mixed with incredulity that any mother could have been so hard and cruel . . . I'm afraid the fluids in her veins have always been as icy cold as they now are in death.'

The coffin travelled through the crowded but silent streets of London to Paddington Station, headed for its final resting place at Windsor. A former Princess of Wales, a former queen and the unquestionable head of her family was being honoured by the nation on her last journey. Marital discord had never entered her experience in the way it had done for many of her predecessors. In this, we may say she had been lucky in finding a partner so well suited to her; or we may say that there was something in her personality and upbringing that ensured the success of her marriage. Mary of Teck was a woman of the nineteenth century living in the twentieth. It was her triumph, as well as her tragedy, that to the last she had put her duty to her country and to her title before everything else in her life.

Diana Spencer (1961–1997)

In the twentieth century, there have been three Princesses of Wales. Of the last, so much has already been said and written that I would not have presumed to add to it, had it not been for her untimely death. I may be accused of sentimentality or hypocrisy, or both, for writing in this way about a woman who, even in death, is almost as widely reviled as she is admired. The fact is that it is almost as unfashionable now to admit to having admired Diana, Princess of Wales as it was, in September 1997, to admit to *not* having admired her.

It is still too early to make a full and impartial assessment of her significance, either for Britain or for Wales. When I first had the idea for this book, I had no thought that she might no longer be living by the time it was published. However, it had already started to look as though her future in the role of Princess of Wales was of limited duration. Her insistence on retaining the title after her divorce took people by surprise, and struck me as the action of an astute and determined woman. If she was to be edged out of the royal family and her marriage against her will, she would at least deter anyone else from filling her role, a role she cherished not for the status it gave her, nor for the adulation of the media, but for the way it enabled her to feel loved by literally millions of ordinary people.

When, as Lady Diana Spencer, she first caught the attention of the newspapers in 1980, few people saw anything out of the ordinary in her, and indeed, there *was* very little. It is easy, with hindsight, to interpret aspects of her early conduct (her response to press attention, for example) as indicative of an out-standingly adept attention-seeker. If we look without prejudice at those photographs and pieces of film and dialogue, all we

Diana, Princess of Wales, touring Canada early in her marriage.
Photograph courtesy of E. Urquhart.

see is a gauche and inexperienced teenager with a pleasant personality, a sense of humour, and not much dress sense. She had not excelled at school, and had the kind of typical teenage interests that had never really been associated with Prince Charles, such as rock music and clothes. One of her main qualifications for the job of Princess of Wales was that she had not had any serious relationships with other men. She was, in short, unspoiled.

Many harsh things have been said about the behaviour of both parties during the marriage of Diana Spencer and Charles, Prince of Wales. In the months before and immediately after the much-celebrated royal wedding of 1981, some expressed doubts as to whether the marriage would last, simply because of the age difference between the two. Others were sceptical about her ability to adapt to the life into which she was marrying. In fact, she carried her personal cross with far more dignity than anyone had a right to expect.

Although it has been claimed that Diana wanted to call off the wedding with a few days to go, it is hardly likely that any nineteen-year-old – especially one with her background – would have had the foresight to turn down the opportunity of becoming Princess of Wales and future Queen of Great Britain; even less likely if she was genuinely fond of the man who made her the proposal. Ordinary people, despite their misgivings, quickly warmed to Diana, and her character was partly formed by their reactions to her. She had the natural advantages of good looks and the ability to wear fashionable clothes with panache, the latter being something few existing members of the royal family possessed.

Although she was the daughter of an earl, and had been part of the same social circle as the prince, her life up to the point of her marriage had been 'normal' in comparison with that of the immediate royal family. Born in 1961 at Park House, next to the queen's Sandringham estate, Diana Spencer was the youngest of three sisters. Diana's parents had divorced when she was six. Her mother had walked out, to live with another man, and a bitter custody battle had followed. The younger children, who loved both parents, must have found this very traumatic; Diana and her younger brother, Charles, were thrown together in unusual circumstances, and drew strength from their intimacy. Their behaviour as adults would appear, superficially at least, to reflect the emotional suffering they endured in childhood.

At school, Diana excelled only at sport. Consequently, she was never forced into an academic career for which she was not suited, and had actually taken a job – as an assistant in a kindergarten. Her lifestyle was in complete contrast to that of the ex-student prince and naval officer. Her older sister Sarah had actually been, briefly, a 'girlfriend' of the Prince of Wales, but Diana herself was closer in age to Prince Andrew, and the possibility of marriage with the queen's middle son had been mentioned, jokingly, within the family. The ultimate prize of the heir to the throne was undreamed of.

Much later, Diana gave Andrew Morton her own account of how Prince Charles proposed. Her immediate response was to think he was joking.

> He said, 'You do realise that one day you will be queen.' And a voice said to me inside, 'You won't be queen, but you'll have a tough role.' So I said, 'Yes.' I said, 'I love you so much, I love you so much.' He said, 'Whatever love means.'

Following the fairy-tale wedding in St Paul's Cathedral, the new Princess of Wales was quickly caught up in the round of royal duties, including a three-day visit to Wales, made with her husband, in October 1981. This was the famous occasion on which she made a stammering attempt at speaking the language, during a ceremony in which she was awarded the freedom of Cardiff. Having managed, 'Y mae'n bleser cael dod i Gymru. Hoffwn dod eto yn fuan. Diolch yn fawr' ('It's a pleasure to be in Wales. I would love to come again. Thank you.'), she went on to add, in English, that she was proud to be Princess of Wales – a staggering statement in the context of traditional royal attitudes towards the principality.

The Prince of Wales had already impressed the population of his adoptive country with his own efforts to learn Welsh by spending a term of undergraduate life at Aberystwyth. It is interesting to note that it had taken until 1969 for this idea to be taken seriously by the monarchy. It had been suggested as long ago as 1632 that Charles Stuart, then Prince of Wales, should learn the language as a signal that he recognized his responsibilities towards the principality. 'If the guardian of your tender youth see fit,' suggested John Davies of Mallwyd in the foreword to his *Dictionarium duplex*, 'Your Highness should be imbued from the cradle, at the same as with other languages, with the ancient language of this island, which is now restricted to your own Welsh people.' Still, better late than never. Now Charles was passing on to his wife what he had learned – not just about the country, but about what would go down well with the locals.

As far as the Welsh were concerned, Diana had made a good start by selecting a Welshman, David Emmanuel, to design her bridal gown. That the dress itself looked crumpled and less than stylish on the wedding day was something that could be overlooked in the excitement. Some recognized the decision on the designer as Diana's own; Buckingham Palace would never have had the imagination to make such a suggestion. Did it mean that she was already taking her responsibilities seriously? Did she recognize the possibility of establishing a special rapport with a nation of three million people, so that, whatever happened in years to come, she would retain her own identity through us? Her biographers are remarkably reticent about her feelings towards Wales, probably because they are looking at her from a peculiarly English point of view.

The first Princess of Wales for seventy years had come home, so to speak, and, despite some minor nationalist activity, that first visit was a great success. On 27 October the *Western Mail* reported both an IRA bomb blast in London and the discovery of an incendiary device at Pontypridd Army Careers Office. By 28 October all this was forgotten as the headlines read, 'Wales opened its heart to royal couple', followed by an account of their whistle-stop tour of north Wales.

Once again, Diana showed her new allegiance, wearing red and green on the first day of the tour, which included a look round Caernarfon Castle where her husband had been invested with his title. The prince, by all accounts, was beginning to be a little put out by all the attention his wife was receiving. One might have expected that here, on his 'home' territory, he could have counted on a little more respect, but he was heard to remark: 'I know my place now.' In photographs, Charles appears in his familiar stance, hands behind back and head bowed, Diana a fraction behind him, looking up nervously at a camera only she has spotted.

In the course of the visit the princess was observed to have a natural way with people. Diana reached into the crowd and touched them; unlike other female royals, she did not wear gloves. The fact that Diana attempted to say 'Diolch yn fawr' ('Thank you'), to those who gave her flowers and gifts, also went down well. On 29 October the princess's increased confidence was becoming apparent in a photograph of her at a Brangwyn Hall concert, wearing an emerald green gown. By now she had received the same rapturous reception in west Wales as she had enjoyed in the north. The following morning, a marvellous press shot shows her waving to onlookers in an upstairs window at Pontypridd, while simultaneously shaking hands with the crowd. The editorial commented that 'the way in which she has coped with three exhausting days, ever ready to give a few more people the chance to shake her hand, has been genuine and heart-warming. Without the training or experience of her husband, she has brought a heightened humanity to the role of royalty.'

At Rhyl, a seven-year-old told Diana that his father had told him to say, 'Give us a kiss', so she did. Her love of children was one thing about Diana Spencer that the media could fasten on, and this they continued to do. When, in due course, she became the mother of Prince William, only a year after her marriage, millions of British women began to identify more closely with her. It became apparent that her fascination with the young would carry through into her private life, and her ideas about how to bring up her children began to mark her out as a special individual. The idea that she should try to teach her two sons about the lives of ordinary people was, if not quite revolutionary, at least unexpected. It would have been so easy for her to enjoy the lifestyle of a Princess of Wales without giving anything back, and she could still have been at least as popular as the rest of the family into which she had married. A 'trusted adviser' of her husband is quoted as saying, unwisely in retrospect, that she 'just seemed to refuse to understand that she was now the Princess of Wales and could not do what she wanted any more'.

Following the example set by the Duchess of Gloucester and Princess Anne, the new Princess of Wales departed from tradition and had both her children in hospital. Though she had herself been brought up by nannies, Diana wanted as normal as possible a start in life for her children. Her official engagements prevented her from spending as much time as she would have liked with William and Harry, so they did have nannies, but of a more modern variety. As soon as decently possible, they went to school, something their father had not done until he was somewhat older. (Even that had been a radical move for the time.) Ludgrove and Eton, boarding schools within easy reach of home, followed.

The relationship between the princess and her 'adopted' country, Wales, grew and developed with the years. Her visits to Wales gave her the opportunity to mix with a race less naturally reserved than the English, and the Welsh appreciated her desire to please. It still seems curious that an upper-class 'English rose' could have been welcomed so warmly by the Welsh, and could have returned that spontaneous warmth, so that we came to think of her, not just as any old princess, but as *ours*. Much the same kind of thing had happened with her husband, Charles, in the days immediately before his investiture at Caernarfon in 1969, but the years between had allowed that relationship to cool. It would become cooler still when he and his wife went their separate ways. It was with the oppressed Diana, not with the well-established Charles, that most Welsh people identified.

The things we know now about the princess's private life have caused us to look at her from a different point of view, but she retains our sympathy if not our admiration. The accusation, publicly made by Penny Junor as an excuse for the behaviour of the prince, that the Princess of Wales was suffering from Borderline Personality Disorder, was picked up from Jonathan Dimbleby. Dimbleby withdrew a chapter on the subject from his 1994 biography of Prince Charles, claiming that the prince's motivation was 'to avoid causing distress to the Princess'. Leading psychiatrists have dismissed the diagnosis, on the grounds that she could not have continued to present such a brave face to the world and carry out her public engagements if she had been suffering from this brand of paranoia.

We know, however, that she had an affair with James Hewitt, aided and abetted by her security staff. We know that she made anonymous telephone calls to Oliver Hoare. It has been alleged that she had affairs with other men, and that she accused the royal nanny, Tiggy Legge-Bourke, of being pregnant by Prince Charles. Thanks in part to the prince's own conscience, we also know the flip side. Another post mortem would serve no purpose.

A telling remark was that made later by Hewitt, to the effect that Diana was not a rebel. In 1990 the princess had allegedly told him that she knew she would never be queen. A divorce between the Prince and Princess of Wales was not something that had never been considered before (remember Caroline of Brunswick's experience) but in the twentieth century the British people had been treated to strong-willed, duty-bound princesses who continued in the same vein when they became queens.

'It made for some great headlines, but divorce was never a real possibility,' wrote Unity Hall in 1991, in her book, *The Private Lives of Britain's Royal Women*. She was eating her words within months, as a separation was announced by Buckingham Palace. When considering the problem, Hall had made some valid points about how such an event would affect Diana and her children. It was said that Diana, if divorced, would remain 'Her Royal Highness', but could not retain the title of Princess of Wales. The opposite happened.

The breakdown of the couple's marriage, whatever its causes, imposed a sense of injury and personal slight on the people of Britain. Scandalous newspaper stories about affairs, rivalry and the princess's eating disorders, which few had believed, turned out to have some truth behind them. Having welcomed Diana into the fold, the public was reluctant to let her go easily. When they learned that some of the blame lay with her, as she admitted in a history-making television interview for the BBC, they were disillusioned, and the media proceeded to get away with cruelty towards Diana, her husband and her children, in the name of the public's right to know.

In the famous *Panorama* interview, the princess commented particularly on how her relationship with the media had affected her marriage. She had waited in vain since the day of her engagement for them to 'go quietly'. Not only did this not happen, but 'it started to focus very much on me, and I seemed to be on the front of a newspaper every single day, which is an isolating experience, and the higher the media put you, the bigger the drop. And I was very aware of that.'

Journalists and photographers have tried to justify themselves by pointing out an apparent inconsistency between Diana's professed reluctance to be photographed and her willingness to use publicity for her own ends. There was no inconsistency. Most of us would like to have our photograph in the paper when we have done something admirable or are being presented with an award, but we always want to be seen at our best. We would not choose to be followed into our homes by a man with a telephoto lens, intent on getting shots of us in bed or in the bath.

Charles himself had foreseen the problems a Princess of Wales might have to face in her dealings with the media. Speaking of the idea of being put on a pedestal, only to be pulled off it, he told an interviewer frankly: 'It frightens me and I know for a fact that it terrifies Diana.'

Diana responded to the furore surrounding her divorce by withdrawing temporarily from public life. Following her separation, she had continued to appear in public as a member of the royal family. Although the prime minister John Major had stated (to Parliament's amazement) that there was no reason why she should not become queen in due course, there was a gradual breaking-down of opposition to the idea of divorce. No one was really surprised when, in July 1996, the Prince and Princess of Wales were granted their decree nisi. Diana immediately dropped her links with over a hundred charities, retaining her connections with only six.

Experts on etiquette proceeded to explain her new status thus:

> On the day her divorce from the Prince of Wales becomes absolute, the Princess of Wales will lose the prefix of 'Her Royal Highness' and will become 'Lady Diana, Princess of Wales'. (The style of 'Lady' is owed to her birth as the daughter of an earl, is unrelated to her status as a member of the Royal Family . . .) Lady Diana, Princess of Wales, to the surprise of many, will no longer be The Princess of Wales, for that is the title of the wife of the man who holds the Principality of Wales of his feudal superior, the Queen. Lady Diana, Princess of Wales, although correctly addressed as such, will not enjoy the title of Princess of Wales.

The title was 'merely a name', just as a divorced wife might continue to call herself 'Mrs Windsor', even if she were no longer married to Mr Windsor or to anyone else. In practice, this meant very little. By the people of Wales, Diana continued to be regarded as their own personal princess. To the nation as a whole, she continued to be 'Princess Diana'.

Writing more prophetically than he knew, A. N. Wilson contrasted the attitudes of the princess and her grandmother-in-law. Whereas Elizabeth Bowes-Lyon had seen herself as 'saviour' of the monarchy in rescuing it from Wallis Simpson, he said, Diana's self-image was 'confused' and she saw herself as a martyr.

In the last year of her life, Diana's relationship with the media became stranger than ever. She continued to shun photographers, and it is believed that she planned to go further and cease all public engagements. This does not fit in well with her stated desire to be 'an ambassador' for Britain and 'princess of *people's* hearts'. What the reaction of those *people* would have been to such a drastic step is difficult to imagine. Had she followed it up by becoming seriously involved with another man, especially a man who was so much an outsider as Dodi Fayed, an Arab millionaire, it is possible that public sympathy would have evaporated. The death of the princess, in a car accident which will never be fully explained, came at a time when she was still widely loved and respected. Guilt can only partly account for the heartfelt and nationally shared mourning that followed.

Diana's funeral is notable because of its context. On her sudden death, royal protocol broke down completely. As a divorced wife, she was, like Katherine of Aragon before her, entitled to no ceremony. Katherine had been better off in that respect, being at least the respectable widow of a former Prince of Wales. What the royal family and its advisers, with the exception of Prince Charles, failed to understand was that they could not rely on existing rules and regulations to deal adequately with a situation that had never before occurred. It seems that the prince had to fight every inch of the way to ensure that his former wife was accorded the dignity and honour expected by the nation.

The funeral, with its unusual elements such as the performance by a prominent rock musician, the outspoken speech by

Diana's younger brother, the applause of the congregation (including the crowds *outside* Westminster Abbey) and finally the burial in a unique resting place designed to keep the princess out of the reach of those who had terrorized her last few years, was an event on which history will look back in awe. Earl Spencer, in his funeral oration, said that '. . . such was her extraordinary appeal that the tens of millions of people taking part in this service all over the world via television and radio who never actually met her, feel that they too lost someone close to them in the early hours of Sunday morning'.

Most fittingly, the service ended with a Welsh hymn tune, 'Cwm Rhondda', and the task of bearing the princess's coffin away from the cathedral was allocated to her own regiment, the Welsh Guards.

A review of earlier chapters makes it only too clear that being a princess is not a recipe for happiness. Diana's tragedy is not unprecedented; it is almost typical. Times have changed, but not that much. Not long before her death, Diana was being compared with Caroline of Brunswick, another Princess of Wales whose conduct drew public comment and scandal. The manner of her death takes us back to the carriage accident which almost claimed Caroline's life in 1806. The parallels between the two women are not as uncanny as they seem; they were the direct result of their position in life. The purpose of this book has not been to draw comparisons between women who held a royal title in vastly different times, but to comment on their position in society and to act as a reminder of the role they played in history.

The Future

It will surprise no one to learn that there is a website dedicated to the life and death of Diana, Princess of Wales. In fact, there are dozens, if not hundreds, of such sites devoted to the subject. Many of their authors clearly have little understanding of the role Diana played in British society. Some may be dismissed by the sophisticated reader as the harmless hobby of people with too much leisure time and imagination. What they all have in common is that they feel a bond of some kind with the late Princess of Wales, that they feel she somehow belonged to them.

There is also a proliferation of books about Diana, Princess of Wales. To add to the many official and unofficial versions of her story that were published in her lifetime, there is a long list of books whose authors each claim a special insight into the history of her life and death. There are semi-factual books on the conspiracy theory, and novels dealing with the investigation of her 'murder'. Leaving aside the fact that Diana was no more murdered than were her rejected predecessors, Katherine of Aragon and Caroline of Brunswick, it cannot be denied that her life has furnished as much material for aspiring writers as has that of any world figure, however long-lived.

It will be a hard act to follow. The Prince of Wales, Diana's former husband, has for years lived openly with a woman to whom he was not married. In British history, as this book illustrates, we find ample precedent for this situation. Even for those reluctant to recognize divorce, the prince was, technically, a widower and consequently free to remarry without any stain on his character in the eyes of the Church, as long as the woman he selected met the required standard.

Therein lies the difficulty. Any future Princess of Wales must be measured against the impossibly high standard set by the last. The curious thing about this is that a new factor has entered the equation, which I call 'the Wales factor'.

In 2002, the BBC held a poll on the subject of 'Great Britons'. Diana, Princess of Wales, narrowly missed winning it, but there was much criticism of her selection even as one of the Top 100. It was open to anyone to vote, and clearly many British people *did* believe her to be worthy. The programme that attempted to assess Diana's greatness was hosted by journalist Rosie Boycott. Not once was Diana's role as Princess of Wales brought into the argument. At no time was her constitutional importance discussed. One might have been forgiven for thinking that the title which gave her a purpose in life had come to mean nothing after her death. That is not true.

In 1936 Edward VIII shocked the nation by selecting as his wife a woman who had been divorced, not once but twice, and who had committed the additional sins of being born American and a commoner. Wallis Simpson was, by most people's standards, quite unsuited to be queen. Before the king acceded to the throne, however, there was relatively little discussion of whether she or any other woman would be suited to the role of Princess of Wales. The job had not had a high profile, even though the king's mother had held the title until 1910.

It is therefore quite surprising that, today, people should be asking not whether Camilla Parker-Bowles is suited to the role of queen, but whether she is suited to the role of Princess of Wales. For her to hold that title would, for many, be a kind of sacrilege.

What does the Princess of Wales do that the queen does not? This is a difficult question, because, for the present, our queen is a monarch in her own right. She can open buildings, launch ships and be a patron of major charities, but she cannot descend from her throne and give up the rights and privileges associated with it. The Princess of Wales, on the other hand, can comfort sick children by putting her arms around them. She can sit on the bed of an Aids victim or attend a rock concert and be seen to enjoy it.

Other 'junior' royals can do much the same, but there is a difference. The Princess Royal, who is now (despite her own divorce and remarriage) widely respected for her hard work and down-to-earth approach, knows that she will never be queen. The Princess of Wales, whoever she may be, marries with an expectation of one day being queen. The example set by Diana Spencer was an extraordinary one, because it led the nation to expect that we would, one day soon, have a queen who had lived an ordinary life and understood ordinary people. Moreover, she was bringing up her sons, the heirs to the throne, to have a similar understanding.

My own daughters took a trip to Techniquest in Cardiff one day, only to find themselves in the company of the two young princes and their mother. Although unable to get really close to the royal party, they did experience something different from their expectations, as no doubt did Prince William and Prince Harry. It goes without saying that the Prince of Wales approved of his sons' mixing with other children and sharing their experiences. For him, the difficulty might have lain in knowing where to draw the line. Although the prince has been, at various times, a schoolboy, a student, a sailor and a business-man, he has never been able to overcome the handicap of being born royal. Diana's achievement was to help his sons to discard that handicap. Her adviser Felix Lyle felt that she 'showed up' the existing monarchy as being completely out of touch with the people.

Assuming that the present Prince of Wales does not marry for a third time, the next Princess of Wales is likely to be the wife of Prince William, when he takes the title on his father's promotion to the throne of Great Britain. Pressure will be put on him to choose well, but the requirements of the royal family will be different from those imposed by public expectation. His mother has set a precedent, a standard for princesses though not for queens.

Whether the institution of marriage will survive is another question. There is as yet little sign of monogamy dying out, and the royal family, assuming it lasts, will be the last to recognize unofficial relationships, even when they exist among its indi-vidual members. It is likely, however, that divorce will become as common for Princes and Princesses of Wales as it is for the population as a whole, and that the idea of a divorced woman becoming a princess will cease to be regarded as scandalous. We will then have come full circle (remember how easily Joan of Kent, the first Princess of Wales, had her marriage annulled).

As for the Welsh, they will continue to want what they have always wanted – a prince and princess who belong specifically to *them*. The next Princess of Wales, in order to succeed in the role, will need to demonstrate an understanding and sympathy for the principality, as it struggles, through its Assembly, to reassert its unique identity within the British Isles. If she plays her cards right, she will have the Welsh people on her side as she confronts the media and the daunting task of living up to Diana's example; that will be no small point in her favour. The population of the rest of the United Kingdom may continue to assume that only what happens in London has real significance. We know better.

Appendix:
Princes of Wales from 1301

Readers may be interested to know about those other Princes of Wales who did not have a Princess. They are, in chronological order:

King Edward II
Prince of Wales 1301–7.
Married Isabella of France in January 1308.

King Edward III
Never formally created Prince of Wales.
Married Philippa of Hainault in January 1328.

King Richard II
Prince of Wales 1376–7
Married (1) Anne of Bohemia in January 1382; (2) Isabella of Valois in November 1396.

King Henry V
Prince of Wales 1399–1413.
Married Katherine of Valois in June 1420.

King Henry VI
Never created Prince of Wales; succeeded to the throne at the age of nine months.
Married Margaret of Anjou in April 1445.

King Edward V
Prince of Wales 1471–83.
Died unmarried, some time in the years 1483–5.

Edward of Middleham
Prince of Wales 1483–4.
Died unmarried; never succeeded to the throne.

King Henry VIII
Prince of Wales 1504–9.
Married Katherine of Aragon in June 1509, two months
after succeeding to the throne.

King Edward VI
Never created Prince of Wales; succeeded to the throne at the
age of ten.
Died unmarried.

Henry Stuart
Prince of Wales 1610–12.
Died unmarried; never succeeded to the throne.

King Charles I
Prince of Wales 1616–25.
Married Henrietta Maria of France in June 1625.

King Charles II
Never formally created Prince of Wales, but called by the title
1638–49.
Married Catherine of Braganza in May 1662. (Some say he
married a Welsh woman, Lucy Walter, while still Prince of
Wales.)

James Francis Edward Stuart
Styled Prince of Wales 1688–1701.
Married Maria Casimire Clementina of Poland in
September 1719, when styled king.

Charles Edward Stuart
Styled Prince of Wales 1720–66.
Married Louise of Stolberg-Gedern in April 1772.

King George III
Prince of Wales 1751–60.
Married Charlotte of Mecklenburg-Strelitz in September 1761.

King Edward VIII
Prince of Wales 1910–36.
Married Wallis Simpson in June 1937.

Select Bibliography

Commynes, Philippe de. *Memoirs*. Penguin, 1972.
Davis, Norman (ed.). *Paston Letters and Papers of the Fifteenth Century* (Clarendon Press, 1971).
Dodington, George Bubb. *Diary of the late George Bubb Dodington* (John Murray, 1823).
Hervey, John, Lord. *Some materials towards memoirs of the Reign of King George II*, ed. Romney Sedgwick (William Kimber, 1952).
Ramm, Agatha (ed.). *Beloved and Darling Child: Last Letters between Queen Victoria and her Eldest Daughter 1886–1901* (Alan Sutton, 1990).
Walpole, Horace. *Memoirs of the Reign of King George II* (Yale University Press, 1985).

Background and general reading

Ashley, Mike. *British Monarchs: The Complete Genealogy, Gazetteer and Biographical Encyclopedia of the Kings and Queens of Britain* (Robinson, 1998).
Dimbleby, Jonathan. *The Prince of Wales: An Intimate Portrait* (Little, Brown, 1994).
Fisher, Deborah C. *Who's Who in Welsh History* (Christopher Davies, 1997).
Foreman, Amanda. *Georgiana, Duchess of Devonshire* (HarperCollins, 1998).
Fraser, Flora. *The Unruly Queen: The Life of Queen Caroline* (Macmillan, 1996).
Hall, Unity. *The Private Lives of Britain's Royal Women* (Michael O'Mara, 1991).

Hough, Richard. *Edward and Alexandra: Their Private and Public Lives* (Hodder & Stoughton, 1992).

Jones, Francis. *The Princes and Principality of Wales* (University of Wales Press, 1969).

Pine, L. G. *Princes of Wales* (David & Charles, 1970 (rev. edn)).

Skidmore, Ian. *Owain Glyndŵr* (Christopher Davies, 1995).

Strickland, Agnes. *Lives of the Queens of England* (Henry Colburn, 1854).

Vaughan-Thomas, Wynford. *The Princes of Wales* (Kaye & Ward, 1982).

Weir, Alison. *Britain's Royal Families: The Complete Genealogy* (Pimlico, rev. edn, 1996).

Fiction

Much historical fiction is inadequately researched and badly written. However, it is sometimes a useful way to gain insight into the life of an era. The novels of Sharon Penman and Jean Plaidy are particularly recommended.

Index